# WAIT UNTIL THE GHOST

### a comedy by Ian Hornby  ©June 1992
### CHARACTERS

| | |
|---|---|
| JACK HARDY | A Solicitor |
| JILLY HARDY | His wife |
| SARAH WATTS | Jilly's best friend |
| EDNA BROWNLOW | Jilly's mother |
| WALTER STERN | Jack's Business Partner |
| INSPECTOR JAMES | A Police Inspector |

*The action of the play passes in the living room of JACK and JILLY HARDY'S single-bedroomed flat.*

| | |
|---|---|
| ACT I | Early one Summer's evening |
| ACT II | Twelve days later - evening |
| ACT III Scene 1 | The following morning |
| ACT III Scene 2 | Half an hour later |

# Wait Until The Ghost Is Clear

## ACT I

*The play is set in the living room of JACK and JILLY HARDY'S one-bedroom flat. The room is furnished in a modern - if inexpensive - style. There is a two-seater bed-settee down L and a matching armchair down R. Down C is a coffee-table on which is a bowl of salted peanuts, which JACK is prone to eat frequently. Up C is a sideboard on which are several bottles of alcoholic drinks and mixers, with glasses. Also on the sideboard is a telephone and a newspaper. In the drawers of the sideboard are some accounts books. On the wall up L is a wall mirror.*

*As the curtain rises JACK is standing down of the settee L. JACK is in his thirties, dressed in smart casual trousers, shirt and sweater. JILLY stands facing him in down of the armchair R. She is slightly younger than Jack, smartly but plainly dressed. They are obviously in the middle of one of their frequent arguments.*

**JACK:** Why the hell does she have to come and stay?

**JILLY:** Why not? She's *my* mother!

**JACK:** Don't remind me...!

**JILLY:** She wants to see me, so why shouldn't she?

**JACK:** But she only lives ten minutes away. And she was only here last month.

**JILLY:** So!? *I* wouldn't complain if you wanted *your* mother to come and stay!

**JACK:** *(Moving L; exasperated)* That's hardly relevant.

**JILLY:** I don't see what the difference is.

**JACK:** My mother's been dead for ten years, that's what!

**JILLY:** What's that got to do with it?

**JACK:** *(Moving R to face Jilly; incredulous)* What's *that* got to do with it...!? Look, I'll admit that the resemblance between your mother and the "living dead" is quite uncanny, but it's hardly the same as me nipping down to the cemetery and digging up *my* Mum to come and stay for a few days, is it!?

**JILLY:** I never made any fuss before she died.

**JACK:** You never *knew* her before she died. We'd not even *met* then, if you remember. *(He sits on the R end of the settee. To himself)* Ah, happy days! *(He takes some peanuts from the bowl and eats them.)*

**JILLY:** It's the principle of the thing. If *your* mother hadn't died, and if I *had* known her, and if you *did* want her to come and stay, and *if* we had the room... *I* wouldn't make a fuss.

**JACK:** *(Standing and moving R)* If, if, if, if.... There's an awful lot of "if"s in your arguments. *(Turning to face Jilly)* The last "if" is the one that gets to me!

**JILLY:** *(Nonchalantly)* Which "if" was that?

**JACK:** You know very well which "if" it was. The one that goes "*If* we had the room"!

**JILLY:** What about it?

**JACK:** We *haven't* got the room!

**JILLY:** We manage.

**JACK:** *(Aghast) We* manage...!? *We*...!? *(Moving L to the settee) Me*, you mean. I don't notice *you* managing! It's not *you* who gets thrown out of your bed and has to sleep on this thing. *(He angrily punches the settee.)*

**JILLY:** *(Aware of what his reaction will be)* It's a big bed... There's room for three. You could always share, if you like.

**JACK:** *(Sitting on the settee)* No thanks! *(Horrified at the thought)* I'd never eat again!

**JILLY:** If you weren't so mean we could have rented a two-bedroomed flat. Then it wouldn't be a problem.

**JACK:** No way! She manages to come and stay often enough when we've only got the one bedroom. If we had two she'd move in permanently.

**JILLY:** *(Sitting on the armchair)* You don't like my mother, do you?

**JACK:** *(Sarcastic)* Whatever gives you that idea?

**JILLY:** *(Coldly)* You make it perfectly obvious!

**JACK:** Rubbish! I worship the very ground she's got coming to her.

**JILLY:** Don't be so horrible...! I'd have done the same for you if your mum was staying.

**JACK:** Oh, my God! Here we go again! She's *dead*, Jilly! She *can't* stay. It's not a fair comparison.

**JILLY:** I bet you'd say the same thing if it was the other way round and it was *my* mother that was dead.

**JACK:** Stop trying to cheer me up.

**JILLY:** It's only for a few days.

**JACK:** *(Suspicious)* How few?

**JILLY:** *(Evasive)* Er... well....

**JACK:** *(More determined)* How few?

**JILLY:** Er... two....

**JACK:** *(He helps himself to some more peanuts. Resigned)* Oh, well, I suppose that's not so bad...

**JILLY:** ... weeks!

**JACK:** *(Choking on his peanuts; dumbfounded)* Two weeks!? Two *whole* weeks!?

**JILLY:** Yes.... Well, seventeen days, actually...

**JACK:** *(Almost speechless)* Seventeen!?

**JILLY:** ...not counting the Sunday and the Tuesday.

**JACK:** *(With foreboding)* What Sunday and Tuesday?

**JILLY:** The day she arrives and the day she leaves.

**JACK:** How you can mention "the day she arrives" in the same tone as "the day she leaves" defeats me.

**JILLY:** *(Puzzled)* What?

**JACK:** *(Grandly)* The first is a black and sorry day. The second is a joyous occasion to be celebrated with liberal quantities of G and T. If she leaves us any, that is.

**JILLY:** And what d'you mean by that!?

**JACK:** Oh, come on, Jilly... If it wasn't for your mother Gordons would be out of business.

**JILLY:** What *are* you going on about?

**JACK:** Forget it.... So this seventeen days is in fact nineteen?

**JILLY:** Well, if you want to put it like that, I suppose it is.

**JACK:** *(Standing and moving L)* I don't *want* to put it like that... that's the way it *is*. *(He turns and faces Jilly.)* And this two weeks, which, when I went to school amounted to fourteen days is, in reality, almost three.

**JILLY:** *(Sulky)* It's only a *bit* more than two.

**JACK:** Jilly, I'm trying very hard to be patient. Two weeks is fourteen days, right?

**JILLY:** Yes, of course.

**JACK:** And three weeks is twenty-one days? Yes?

**JILLY:** Yes.

**JACK:** And your mother's here for nineteen days. Nineteen less fourteen is five, and twenty-one less nineteen is two, which means it's much closer to three weeks than two!

**JILLY:** It's near enough. You know I'm no good at percentages.

**JACK:** *(He turns L. Shaking his head; full of gloom and doom)* Three bloody weeks!

**JILLY:** Jack! Language!

**JACK:** *(Turning to face her; looking for a fight)* Three whole *bloody* weeks!

**JILLY:** *(Trying to be helpful)* Less two days.

**JACK:** Only two days off for good behaviour! *(He moves to the settee.)*

**JILLY:** *(Dismissive)* It'll fly by.

**JACK:** The only thing that'll fly by is your mother.... On her broomstick!
*(He sits.)*
**JILLY:** You're just being stupid, now.
**JACK:** That's easy for you to say. You haven't got to sleep on this bloody thing. *(He thumps the settee.)*
**JILLY:** It's not that bad.
**JACK:** How d'you know? Have you ever slept on it?
**JILLY:** No...
**JACK:** Well, then.
**JILLY:** ...But I often sit on it and watch the telly. It's quite comfy, really.
**JACK:** What the hell has *that* got to do with it? I often *sit* on my bike, but I wouldn't want to sleep on it!
**JILLY:** You're being stupid again. It's quite a comfy settee.
**JACK:** Comfy *settee* it may be... comfy *bed* it definitely is not.
**JILLY:** *(Standing)* You're just *determined* to cause trouble, aren't you?
**JACK:** Not me! *I* didn't invite *my* mother to stay.
**JILLY:** No. As you pointed out, she's dead. And the way you're behaving I'm beginning to wish it was hereditary.
*(JILLY picks up the bowl of peanuts and offers them to JACK.)*
**JILLY:** Have a peanut.
**JACK:** I don't want a bloody peanut!
*(JILLY slams the bowl back on the table and turns R. After a moment JACK helps himself absent-mindedly to some peanuts and chews them idly.)*
**JACK:** *(After a pause)* So you reckon this settee's comfortable, do you?
**JILLY:** Yes.
**JACK:** In that case, why can't *she* sleep on it?
**JILLY:** Mum?
**JACK:** Yes. Her! Or is that sort of thing beneath her?
**JILLY:** Now you're really being ridiculous. She's far too old.
**JACK:** *I'm* far too old. Or at least I feel it!
**JILLY:** Pity you don't act it. Anyway, you're not as old as my mother!
**JACK:** That's true. Nobody's that old!
**JILLY:** *(Angry)* Will you stop insulting my mother!?
**JACK:** Will she stop coming to visit?
**JILLY:** No!
**JACK:** Then *I* won't stop insulting her.
**JILLY:** You're bloody infuriating at times, Jack.

## Wait Until The Ghost Is Clear

JACK: *(Not sorry at all)* Terribly sorry.

JILLY: No you're not! If *you* weren't sleeping on that settee tonight I'd.... *(lost for words)* I'd make you sleep on that settee tonight. *(She turns R.)* Even that's too good for you.

JACK: Surprised you don't want me to sleep in the bath!

JILLY: Don't tempt me!

*(JACK stretches along the settee and looks uncomfortable.)*

JACK: "Comfy"!? There's a bar right across the middle of my back. Be the death of me, this thing.

JILLY: At least that'd shut you up.

JACK: Oh, I see. Planning my demise, eh?

JILLY: Sometimes I think it'd be worth it. You're well insured.

JACK: No. You'd miss me. You'd have nobody's life to make a misery. Nobody to shout at.

JILLY: *(Dreamily)* Heaven.

*(After a pause, JACK stands and moves behind Jilly. He touches her arm.)*

JACK: *(Conciliatory)* Oh, hell, Jilly. Let's not argue again.

JILLY: *(Shaking free of his arm)* Again!? That implies we stopped at some time!

JACK: Please...

JILLY: *(Rounding on him)* Then stop insulting my mother! *(She moves L.)*

JACK: *(Following)* I'm sorry. I can't help it. She asks for it.

JILLY: *(Spinning to confront him)* No she doesn't! It's *you*...! You're totally self-centred! You, you, you! All you ever think about! You never even consider anyone else.

JACK: Now, Jilly, that's not fair.

JILLY: Fair or not, it's true! It doesn't matter that *I* want to see my mother. It doesn't matter that my mother wants to see *me*. All that matters is that *you're* not inconvenienced for a couple of days.

JACK: Nineteen.

JILLY: *(Blazing)* Alright! Alright! Nineteen bloody days..! When we were first married you'd have slept on that settee for a year if I'd asked you to.

JACK: We didn't have that settee when we got married. Your mother bought it for us when we moved here. At the time I thought she was being generous. Now I know the truth!

JILLY: You know what I mean! *(A slight pause.)* It's gone, Jack.... All gone.

JACK: *(Puzzled)* The settee?

**JILLY:** Our marriage! The romance! We lost it somewhere along the way.

**JACK:** Now don't talk like that, Jilly. You know I hate it when you talk like that.

**JILLY:** But it's true, Jack. Can't you see?

**JACK:** No, I can't.

**JILLY:** When was the last time you told me you love me?

**JACK:** Now don't start that again. It's not fair. I've told you before - men don't say things like that.

**JILLY:** Bollocks!

**JACK:** And women *shouldn't* say things like that.

**JILLY:** *(Advancing on him; taunting)* Bollocks....! Bollocks! Bollocks! All *bollocks*!

**JACK:** It's not... "bollocks". It's true. But what I mean is... just because I don't *say* it doesn't mean I don't *mean* it, if you get what I mean.

**JILLY:** You're not even making sense now!

**JACK:** You know what I.... mean.

**JILLY:** Say it now.

**JACK:** What?

**JILLY:** Say it now. Tell me you love me.

**JACK:** But... I can't just come out with it like that.

**JILLY:** Coward!

**JACK:** And even if I did, it wouldn't mean anything if it was forced, would it?

**JILLY:** *Coward!*

**JACK:** *(Reacting)* I am *not* a coward!

**JILLY:** Say it, then!

**JACK:** *(Almost pleading)* But Jilly...!

*(They are now face-to-face.)*

**JILLY:** *(Screaming)* SAY IT!

**JACK:** *(Shouting; at the end of his tether)* Alright... I love you, you stupid bloody cow!

**JILLY:** That sounded *really* convincing. "I love you you stupid bloody cow!" Who said romance was dead?

**JACK:** *(Still angry)* I meant... mean it!

**JILLY:** *(Sarcastic)* Sounds like it.

**JACK:** *(Calmer)* I didn't mean it to sound like *that*, that's all. You got me annoyed.

**JILLY:** Good! About time you had a taste of your own medicine.

## Wait Until The Ghost Is Clear

**JACK:** What d'you mean?

**JILLY:** About time someone got *you* annoyed. That's what *you* do to *me*, you know. Morning, noon and every bloody night. You get me annoyed. I lose my temper. I get a headache. I can't sleep. It puts me off my food. *(Pause)* And I HATE it! *(She turns L.)*

**JACK:** But, darling... I don't do it deliberately.

**JILLY:** *(Turning R; enraged)* Well you're bloody good at it! And don't call me "darling" unless you mean it!

*(They stare at each other, their faces inches apart, for several moments until their rage subsides. JACK is the first to back away, and JILLY also relaxes slightly.)*

**JACK:** *(Genuinely repentant)* I'm sorry.

**JILLY:** *(Facing him again; ready to continue the fight)* You're sorry!? You're bloody *sorry*!?

**JACK:** *(Standing up to her again)* That's what I said. I'm sorry!

*(They stare at each other again, their faces inches apart, for several moments. Eventually JILLY realises he really is sorry and there is nothing to be gained by continuing the fight. They gradually relax.)*

**JILLY:** *(Sitting in the armchair)* Then I accept your apology.

**JACK:** You do?

**JILLY:** Yes.

**JACK:** *(Ingratiating)* Promise?

**JILLY:** *(A hint of hostility)* Don't push it, Jack. Just leave it.

**JACK:** Sorry, Jilly. And.... *(He stops.)*

**JILLY:** What?

**JACK:** *(Quietly)* I do.

**JILLY:** You *do* what?

**JACK:** I do love you.

**JILLY:** *(A hint of sarcasm)* Good God! He said it.

**JACK:** Don't be cruel. I'm trying to make up.

**JILLY:** Yes... My turn to apologise.

**JACK:** Yes. *(He sits on the settee.)*

*(They are silent for a few moments. All of a sudden JILLY leaps up, points towards the lower wall up L and screams.)*

**JACK:** *(Startled)* What's the matter!?

**JILLY:** *(Petrified)* It's... it's... the spider!

**JACK:** *(Relieved)* Oh, is that all?

**JILLY:** Get rid of it! Get rid of it! You know I hate them.

## Wait Until The Ghost Is Clear

**JACK:** *(Moving L and searching)* All right, all right.
**JILLY:** But don't kill it.
**JACK:** Where did it go?
**JILLY:** I don't know. Find it!
**JACK:** *(On his knees searching)* All right, keep your hair on...! I can't see it. It must run off.
**JILLY:** I wish you'd get it. You know I hate spiders.
**JACK:** They won't hurt you.
**JILLY:** I know. They just scare me.

*(JACK stands and shakes his head. They are silent for a few moments. JILLY sits on her armchair.)*

**JILLY:** *(Attempting to calm the atmosphere)* No more rows?
**JACK:** No.
**JILLY:** And no more insults?
**JACK:** No. I promise. I won't insult you again. Or at least I'll try not to.

*(He sits on the settee.)*

**JILLY:** I'll remind you you said that.
**JACK:** I mean it. I'll try.
**JILLY:** And my mother?
**JACK:** What about her?
**JILLY:** You won't insult her either?
**JACK:** Ah, now, wait a minute. This agreement's between you and me, not that old...
**JILLY:** *(Stopping his flow)* Jack! It's all or nothing.
**JACK:** *(He takes a deep breath.)* Very well.
**JILLY:** Promise me.
**JACK:** Now, Jilly, don't be childish.
**JILLY:** Promise me. She'll be here any minute. Promise me.
**JACK:** O.K! O.K! I promise!

*(The doorbell rings off R. JILLY stands and moves R.)*

**JACK:** That'll be the old cow now.

*(JILLY turns to him, her face like thunder.)*

**JACK:** *(Standing; realising a hasty retreat is in order)* I'm going to the loo. *(He grabs the paper and moves towards the door L.)*

*(The doorbell rings again. JILLY exits R. The front door is heard to open off R. JACK opens the door L to leave, but when he hears Sarah's voice he closes it and enters again.)*

**SARAH:** *(Off L)* Hi, Jilly. I was just wondering if you...

## Wait Until The Ghost Is Clear

**JILLY:** *(Off L; obviously delighted)* Sarah! Come on in!

**SARAH:** No, I don't want to disturb you if you're....

**JILLY:** You're not disturbing us. Go through.

*(SARAH enters R and moves down C, followed by JILLY, who moves down R. SARAH is the same age as Jilly. She is very attractive, has immaculate hair and is very sexily and tastefully dressed, although she retains an innocent air. JACK's attitude betrays the fact that he finds her incredibly attractive, but she seems unaware of his attraction for her.)*

**JILLY:** *(Seeing Jack has returned)* I thought you were going to the....

**JACK:** *(Hiding his paper quickly behind him and cutting Jilly off before she can say "toilet" in front of Sarah)* Changed my mind.

**JILLY:** *(Making the point anyway)* Toilet.

**JACK:** *(Moving towards Sarah. Ingratiating)* Hello, Sarah.

**SARAH:** I was just saying to Jilly, I don't want to disturb you if you're...

**JILLY:** And I told her she wasn't disturbing us.

**JACK:** *(His look betrays the fact that she disturbs him considerably and he pauses before replying while he considers what he would like to say.)* No. Of course not. You're not disturbing *me* at all.

**JILLY:** Anyway, you were saying...?

**SARAH:** Yes, I was wondering if Jack could have a look at my hair dryer. I'm useless with electrical gadgets. You're dead lucky to have a man about the house.

**JILLY:** *(Sarcastic)* Yes... Aren't I just?

**JACK:** What's wrong with it?

**SARAH:** I don't know. It just stopped working. I'd just got out of the shower and was drying my hair when it stopped. Damned nuisance. There I was, standing there in just my bra and knickers, hair all wet, and no hair dryer. I'm sure you can imagine what a nuisance it was.

**JACK:** *(Imagining something else altogether; hot under the collar)* Oh, yes. I can imagine alright!

**JILLY:** *(Well aware of how attractive Jack finds Sarah)* Yes, I *bet* you can. I'm sure Jack could manage to spare you a few minutes, couldn't you, Jack? *(She sits in the armchair.)*

**JACK:** *(Trying to be nonchalant, but obviously very keen on the idea)* Yes, I can probably spare you an hour or two. As a matter of fact I'm fairly free now. Shall I come back to your flat with you and I could...

**SARAH:** Oh, I couldn't trouble you now.

**JACK:** It's no trouble.... honestly! Shall we go? *(He moves towards the door R.)*

## Wait Until The Ghost Is Clear

SARAH: Well, we don't need to go back to my flat.
JACK: *(Disappointed)* We don't? *(He moves a step L.)*
SARAH: No. I thought you'd say you'd help me, so I took the liberty of putting it in the car.
JACK: *(Glum)* Oh, good. Very thoughtful.
SARAH: Shall I go and get it?
JILLY: Yes, Sarah. I should.
*(SARAH breezes off R. JACK watches her go.)*
JILLY: *(Advancing on Jack)* D'you have to make it so bloody obvious?
JACK: What?
JILLY: You know very well what. If your eyes had been any farther out of their sockets they'd have popped out and rolled under the settee.
JACK: Nonsense! *(He moves L.)*
JILLY: I remember when you used to look at *me* like that.
JACK: *(Sotto voce; glum)* I don't.
JILLY: *(Realising what he has said)* What!?
JACK: Er.. I *don't*... I don't look at Sarah like anything.
JILLY: Huh!
JACK: I can't help it if I find her attractive. I am a man, after all.
JILLY: That's nothing to boast about.
JACK: *(Vain)* Anyway, I like to think the feeling is mutual. *(He sits on the settee.)*
JILLY: *(Incredulous)* What!?
JACK: I like to think Sarah finds me attractive as well.
JILLY: I don't believe I'm hearing this! Sarah comes here to visit *me*, her best friend. If it wasn't for the fact that every time she does your tongue is hanging out like some horrible purple hearth-rug, she wouldn't even know *you* exist.
JACK: She came round to see me, didn't she?
JILLY: Only because she wants her hair dryer fixed and she knows she only has to give a little flash of her eyes for you to agree to anything.
JACK: *(With deliberate lecherous double-meaning)* Nothing wrong with her giving me a quick flash every now and again.
JILLY: So help me! You've got a mind like a sewer.
JACK: *(Innocently)* Don't know what you mean.
JILLY: I somehow wonder how she manages to retain this air of total naivety she has. Most women can spot your sort miles away. If she *wasn't* so damned unaware of it I could really get to hate her. Although I sometimes

wonder if she isn't more aware then we give her credit for.
*(SARAH enters R, carrying a hair dryer. JACK stands. SARAH gives the hairdryer to Jack, along with a beaming smile.)*

**SARAH:** D'you think you can fix it?

**JACK:** Yes, I'll have a look at it tomorrow. *(He puts the hairdryer on the sideboard.)*

**SARAH:** *(Disappointed)* Oh.

**JILLY:** Something wrong?

**SARAH:** Well, I was sort of hoping that you could look at it now. I'm going out tonight and my hair's a right mess. *(She passes her hand through her immaculate hair.)*

**JACK:** *(Defending her)* Oh, no, I wouldn't say that...

**JILLY:** *(Cutting him dead; matter-of-fact)* Your hair looks fine... as always.

**JACK:** I'm supposed to be doing some work tonight, but I could do it tomorrow if it's really....

**JILLY:** *(Curt)* No you won't! *(To Sarah)* You can borrow mine for tonight. Jack can sort yours out tomorrow.

**JACK:** Yes, and then I could drop it round at your flat if you like.

**JILLY:** There's no need. Sarah's coming round in the morning to see my mother.

**JACK:** *(Sotto voce; to Sarah)* Go to the zoo... It's cheaper.

**SARAH:** Pardon?

**JILLY:** Ignore him. I'll get the dryer. *(She moves towards the door L. As she passes Jack, sotto voce)* And you.... behave! *(She exits L.)*

*(JACK is like a nervous teenager. SARAH smiles at him. There is an uneasy silence while he tries to think of something witty to say, but cannot. Eventually he just grins back.)*

**JACK:** So.... *(He can think of nothing more to say.)*

**SARAH:** What?

**JACK:** What...? Oh, er... nothing.

*(JACK picks up the peanuts.)*

**JACK:** *(Offering them to Sarah)* Nut?

**SARAH:** Yes, thanks.

**JACK:** *(Handing her the bowl)* Here... help yourself.

**SARAH:** Thanks. *(She toys with the nuts. After a pause)* Jack....

**JACK:** *(Glad the silence is broken)* Yes?

**JILLY:** I hope you won't mind me asking, but...

**JACK:** Ask away.
**SARAH:** Have you and Jilly been having a row?
**JACK:** Is there a "y" in the day?
**SARAH:** I thought I could sense an atmosphere.
**JACK:** Her mother's coming to stay.
**SARAH:** Yes, she told me, remember? I'm coming round to see her tomorrow.
**JACK:** Why put yourself through that sort of punishment?
**SARAH:** Edna's not that bad.
**JACK:** You need your eyes tested.
**SARAH:** She's going on holiday.
**JACK:** *(Perking up)* Is she? I didn't know.
**SARAH:** Yes, she's going for a week to Spain.
**JACK:** A week's not *nearly* long enough...
**SARAH:** *(Puzzled)* What...?
**JACK:** It should do wonders for Anglo-Spanish relations!
**SARAH:** I went to the same resort last year. She wants to see my holiday snaps, to see what the place is like. Not that they'll do her much good. I don't take many scenic shots. Most of them are of me lounging about in my bikini. Dreadfully boring.
**JACK:** *(His imagination aflame again)* Yes, they sound it.
*(They are silent for a few moments. JACK gets an idea.)*
**JACK:** Sarah...
**SARAH:** Mmmm?
**JACK:** I was thinking.... I could quite fancy a Spanish holiday myself. This resort you stayed in.... What was it like?
**SARAH:** Very nice. Good beaches, nice hotels. A bit crowded, but then most of them are.
**JACK:** Oh, I....
**SARAH:** Tell you what! Why not have a look at my photos? I've got them with me.
**JACK:** *(As if the thought had never occurred to him)* That's a good idea. Why didn't *I* think of that?
*(SARAH places the nuts on the table, sits and opens her bag. She takes out a folder of photographs. Jack sits on the settee opposite her and she starts to hand him the photos one by one, explaining each as she does so.)*
**SARAH:** That's me by the hotel pool. It was really hot that day.
*(JACK looks wide-eyed at the photograph and mops his brow as if he, too, is*

## Wait Until The Ghost Is Clear

*really hot.)*
**JACK:** Yes, it is, isn't it?
**SARAH:** And this one is on the main beach.
**JACK:** *(Agog)* Very nice.
**SARAH:** I had to get rid of that bikini.
*(JILLY enters L, unseen by Jack. She carries a hair-dryer and quickly takes in the scene.)*
**JACK:** *(In a strangled voice)* Why? It's really... nice.
**SARAH:** Yes, but it turned transparent when it got wet. *(She starts to hand him another photograph)* Look, you can see in this one where I'm coming out of the sea....
**JILLY:** *(Stepping in quickly, and grabs the photograph and pushes the hairdryer into Sarah's hand)* Here you are, Sarah. You'll be wanting to go home and get ready, won't you? *(She snatches the other photos from Jack and gives them back to Sarah. Lying)* Your hair's in an awful state!
**SARAH:** *(Rising)* Is it..!? *(She looks in the mirror and adjusts her hair.)* Yes, I suppose I better had.
*(SARAH puts the photos back in the wallet and then in her bag.)*
**JILLY:** *(To Sarah; with menace)* I'll talk to *you* tomorrow.
**JACK:** *(Hoping to stop her going)* You could stay if you like... Edna should be here any minute.
**JILLY:** *(Adamant; urging her R)* No, Mum'll be tired.
**JACK:** *(Hopefully)* D'you want to leave the photos and I'll give them to Edna?
**JILLY:** *(Hostile)* No... She doesn't! Mum can see them tomorrow.
**SARAH:** *(Apparently oblivious to the menace in Jilly's voice)* Yes, O.K. About ten?
**JILLY:** *(Pointedly)* Make it eleven. Jack'll be out at the Club by then.
**SARAH:** *(Cheerily)* O.K. See you. Thanks for the dryer. See you, Jack.
**JACK:** Yes. 'Bye, Sarah.
*(SARAH exits R, followed by JILLY. There are one or two muffled angry words from JILLY off R and corresponding muffled words of defence from SARAH. JACK sits, his mind is elsewhere so the words off R do not register. The front door is heard to slam and JILLY enters R.)*
**JILLY:** The scheming little bitch!
**JACK:** *(Surprised)* Who?
**JILLY:** You know bloody well who! And I could kill *you*!
**JACK:** *Me*? What have *I* done?

## Wait Until The Ghost Is Clear

**JILLY:** Drooling over her photographs like that!
**JACK:** *(Innocent)* She was just showing me where she went in Spain last year.
**JILLY:** I know very well what she was showing you. And it had nothing to do with Spain. Little tramp!
**JACK:** I thought she was your best friend?
**JILLY:** So did I! Shows how wrong you can be about people.
**JACK:** How d'you mean?
**JILLY:** She knew perfectly well what she was doing!
**JACK:** And what exactly *was* she doing?
**JILLY:** Flaunting herself, that's what.
**JACK:** Just 'cause she showed me her photos?
**JILLY:** They weren't ordinary photos.
**JACK:** *(Without thinking)* You can say that again.
**JILLY:** There! See what I mean. Just as well you've got a strong heart. I could hear your heart thumping as soon as I walked into the room.
**JACK:** I'm sure she wouldn't.... Not to me... I mean, you said she doesn't even know I exist.
**JILLY:** Like I said.... How wrong can you be?
**JACK:** *(He is pleased with the idea. He stands, moves L, then turns to face her.)* D'you really think she fancies me?
**JILLY:** *(Enraged)* Jack!
**JACK:** Sorry!
**JILLY:** She was playing games with you. You and every other man I bet.
**JACK:** You're very quick to condemn her. It was only five minutes ago you said she was as white as white.
**JILLY:** Yes. Now I know the truth... she's as scarlet as Scarlett.
**JACK:** I think you're imagining things.
**JILLY:** *I* don't.
**JACK:** *(After a pause; taunting)* I know what it is... You're jealous!
**JILLY:** Don't flatter yourself!
**JACK:** *(Moving towards Jilly)* You are! Admit it!
**JILLY:** I am not!
**JACK:** *I* don't know! Typical woman! Normally you can't stand the sight of me, but as soon as someone half attractive - and Sarah isn't half attractive...
**JILLY:** Pig!
**JACK:** As soon as that happens you get all protective and your claws come

15

out!
JILLY: So what if they do!?
JACK: Why do *you* care!? A few minutes ago you were going to cash me in for my life insurance.
JILLY: What if I was? I'm damned if *she's* getting her talons on the money!
JACK: *(Shaking his head in disbelief)* You, jealous! I never thought I'd see the day.
JILLY: You'd be exactly the same if the situation was reversed.
JACK: Why? Who d'you think would fancy *you*?
JILLY: *(Standing; hurt)* You bastard!
JACK: Temper, temper!
JILLY: You'd love to get rid of me, wouldn't you? What the hell's wrong with you today? You're determined to have a fight, aren't you?
JACK: Me!? You're the one who's caused all the trouble.
JILLY: All *I* did was invite Mum to stay.
JACK: There you are, then.
JILLY: Urrrgh! I don't believe you!
JACK: *(Moving L)* I'm going to get my pistol.
JILLY: Good! Perhaps it'll go off and do us all a favour.
JACK: No, don't worry. I won't be pointing it at your mother.
*(The doorbell rings off R.)*
JILLY: Ah, speak of the.... *(She stops, realising what she was about to say.)*
JACK: *(He stops and turns to face her. Finishing for her; deliberately)* ...Devil!?
*(JILLY gives him a withering look and exits R. The front door is heard to open.)*
EDNA: *(Off R)* Oh, Gillian, *darling*, my feet are killing me.
JACK: Damn! *I* wanted to do it!
JILLY: Never mind, Mum. Come in and take the weight off them.
*(JACK shakes his head and exits L. EDNA and JILLY enter R. EDNA is in her sixties. She wears a smart suit and a permanent superior expression. She talks with a snobby voice and is frequently given to making observations to nobody in particular. She carries three carrier bags which she puts on the floor at the upstage end of the settee and then she sits on the settee. She takes off her shoes and massages her feet.)*
EDNA: Phew! I think I'm getting old, Gillian. I'm worn out carrying those bags.

| | |
|---|---|
| JILLY: | What's wrong with your car? |
| EDNA: | Nothing, darling.... Why? |
| JILLY: | Why didn't you bring it? |
| EDNA: | I did... It tired me out carrying the bags from the car. |
| JILLY: | Where's your case? |
| EDNA: | My *cases* are in the car, dear. Perhaps that... *(with disrespect)* husband of yours... |
| JILLY: | *(Sensing Edna's disrespect)* Jack? |
| EDNA: | *(With distaste)* Yes.., *Jack*. Never did like him. Perhaps *he* could bring them in. |
| JILLY: | *(Sure he wouldn't; moving L)* I'm sure he'd *love* to. *(Opening the door L and calling)* Jack! |
| JACK: | *(Off L; gruff)* What? |
| JILLY: | *(Calling)* Can you get Mum's cases out of the car? |
| JACK: | *(Off L)* No! I'm busy! |
| JILLY: | *(In warning tones)* Jack...! Remember what we said. |
| JACK: | *(Resigned)* Oh, alright. Just coming. |

*(JILLY moves R and sits in the armchair.)*

JILLY: He's just coming.

*(After a few moments. JACK enters unhurriedly L. He is carrying a pistol which he is cleaning with a cloth. As he enters he stops just inside the door, mentally prepares himself, takes a deep breath, adopts a beaming smile, then goes to Edna.)*

| | |
|---|---|
| JACK: | *(Artificially pleasant)* Edna! How nice to see you! You look wonderful. *(He kisses her on the cheek and stands up C.)* |
| EDNA: | *(By way of explanation)* I've just got back from the beauty salon. |
| JACK: | Oh, really? When are they going to be able to start the work? |
| JILLY: | *(Warning)* Jack...! |
| JACK: | Yes, it's wonderful to see you... it seems *ages* since you were last here. |
| JILLY: | Alright, Jack! Don't overdo it. |
| JACK: | *(Sitting on the upstage arm of the settee; ignoring Jilly)* Jilly tells me you're coming to stay for a couple of days. |
| EDNA: | A *few* days, yes. I thought she needed some help around the flat. |
| JACK: | How kind of you. Isn't she kind, Jilly? I mean... *(Sarcastic)* there's such a lot of work in this flat, what with this *enormous* lounge, the kitchen, a bathroom, the toilet - a *separate* toilet, don't forget, and that *huge* bedroom. |
| JILLY: | Jack...! |

**JACK:** That *one* huge bedroom, with that *one* double bed just *made* for a married couple.

**EDNA:** I know you don't want me here, Jack. You've always made it *perfectly* obvious.

**JACK:** *(Innocent)* Me?

**EDNA:** But I've got to look after my daughter. She's all I have.

**JACK:** She can look after herself, believe me.

**EDNA:** I expect she has to. From what she tells me *you're* precious little help. Now, put that... that *toy* down and get my bags.

**JACK:** *(Defending his pistol)* It is *not* a toy. This is a piece of precision engineering, made by craftsmen from decades of experience.

**EDNA:** I fail to see why grown men have to play with guns, anyway.

**JACK:** I don't play with it. I shoot it.

**EDNA:** Dangerous if you ask me. Having a gun in the flat. Someone could get hurt.

**JACK:** It is *not* dangerous. I have a licence for it and I know how to handle it.

**EDNA:** These are dreadful times. Anyone could break in and steal it.

**JILLY:** *(Tiring of the argument)* They can't, Mum. Jack has to keep it in a special metal safe which is set in concrete in the kitchen wall. The Police inspected it before he got the licence.

**JACK:** *(Staggered at Jilly's support)* Thank you, Jilly.

**EDNA:** Well *I* still think it's childish. Cowboys and Indians!

**JACK:** I'll have you know I'm a very good shot. I find the whole thing very therapeutic.

**EDNA:** Is that another word for pathetic?

**JACK:** You should be flattered, Edna - I *always* think of you when I'm shooting. *(He stands.)*

**EDNA:** Hah! I don't believe *that*. All *you* ever think of is yourself!

**JACK:** Believe it!

**EDNA:** *(Taking some keys from her pocket and handing them to Jack)* There are three cases in the boot and two on the back seat. And while you're there you can bring in the carrier bags from the front seat.

**JACK:** *(Placing his pistol on the sideboard)* Travelling light again, eh?

**EDNA:** *(To Jilly)* I've bought us some steaks for tea. Build you up a bit.

**JILLY:** We were going to have an Indian take-away.

**EDNA:** You don't want to go eating that *foreign* muck. It's bad for you.

**JACK:** *(Moving up C)* How d'you work that out?

## Wait Until The Ghost Is Clear

**EDNA:** You only have to look at the Indians to see what I mean. I've seen them on the television. Running about with red faces shooting bows and arrows and wearing nothing but a fragment of cloth. I've seen them! It's all that foreign food that does it! Sends you mad.

**JACK:** *(Shaking his head in disbelief)* I give up. *(He exits R.)*

**EDNA:** Big kids!

**JILLY:** Who? Indians?

**EDNA:** *(With meaning)* No.., cowboys. Jack and that friend of his... what's his name?

**JILLY:** Walter?

**EDNA:** Yes, Walter. He's another one, isn't he?

**JILLY:** Another solicitor? Yes, he's Jack's partner.

**EDNA:** Another *cowboy*! Playing with guns.

**JILLY:** Oh... yes.

*(The telephone rings. JILLY rises and answers it.)*

**EDNA:** *(Muttering)* Big kids!

**JILLY:** Hello, 747 3949..... Oh, hello, Walter. Your ears must have been burning. We were just talking about you.... No, *all* bad... No.. He's getting some of Mum's bags out of her car. D'you want me to shout him...? Tonight? Yes, I don't see why not. He's just been cleaning his gun, so I suppose... Nine o'clock... O.K. I'll tell him.... 'Bye, Walter. *(She replaces the receiver. To Edna)* That was Walter.

**EDNA:** I guessed.

**JILLY:** He wants Jack to go to the shooting club with him. *(She moves to the armchair and sits.)* That's where he and Jack first met, you know... at the shooting club. They enjoy it.

**EDNA:** I suppose it keeps them quiet.

**JILLY:** I quite like Walter.

**EDNA:** Is he married?

**JILLY:** No, I don't think so.

**EDNA:** Wealthy?

**JILLY:** I've no idea!

**EDNA:** Must cost a fortune, buying all these guns and so on.

**JILLY:** Don't remind me! Walter and Jack spent over three thousand pounds on those pistols.

**EDNA:** *(Aghast)* Three thousand!?

**JILLY:** Yes. They're an identical pair.

**EDNA:** Yes, a pair of idiots!

19

| | |
|---|---|
| JILLY: | They *had* to have the same. You know what men are like. |
| EDNA: | Yes, don't I just? |

*(JACK enters R laden with suitcases which he carries L. The door is closed and he has to put the cases down to open it. JILLY and EDNA watch him.)*

| | |
|---|---|
| JACK: | *(Sarcastic)* No! Don't get up. I can manage! *(He picks up the case and struggles off L.)* |
| EDNA: | He's got a funny attitude, that one. |
| JILLY: | I know. I don't know what's the matter with him. |
| EDNA: | Runs in the family. |
| JILLY: | *(Puzzled)* What..? |
| EDNA: | He's just like your father. |
| JILLY: | Who, Jack..? But he's no relation to Dad. |
| EDNA: | Anyone would think he was. You can really see the resemblance. |
| JILLY: | What? Between Jack and Dad? |
| EDNA: | Yes. Like peas in a pod. Another big kid! |
| JILLY: | Who? |
| EDNA: | Your father. Messing about in the loft all day with a child's train set, would you believe? Spent all day and half the night up there. I can't think why. It was dreadful trying to get up that stupid ladder. *I* could never manage it. |

*(JACK enters L and crosses R.)*

| | |
|---|---|
| JACK: | *(As he passes)* Only a few more trips. |
| EDNA: | It's taking you long enough. |
| JACK: | I had trouble getting in. There was so much luggage the car door was below the kerb. I had to jack it up to get it open. *(He exits R to get more luggage.)* |
| JILLY: | What did you do with Dad's train sets after he died? |
| EDNA: | They're still up there. I told you.. *I* can't get up there... He left them to me in his will, you know. |
| JILLY: | Yes, you said. |
| EDNA: | Sarcasm...! A stupid idea. I bet he only did it out of spite. *(A pause)* A pity *you* didn't have kids. |
| JILLY: | *(Wearily)* Oh, Mum... Don't start that again. |
| EDNA: | Well.... I like children. I'd have had more if I hadn't had all that trouble when I had you. Your father said he didn't want to risk it again. Thoughtful of him, I suppose. |
| JILLY: | *(Having heard it all before)* Yes, Mum. |
| EDNA: | It would have been wonderful if you could have given me some |

grandchildren.

**JILLY:** *(Slightly snappy)* Well we can't, and that's all there is to it!

**EDNA:** The end of the line, you know.

**JILLY:** What?

**EDNA:** The end of the line. No more Brownlows.

**JILLY:** They wouldn't have been Brownlows. They would have been Hardys.

**EDNA:** That's beside the point! *(A pause.)* There's still time, you know.

**JILLY:** Time for what?

**EDNA:** To have some grandchildren.

**JILLY:** *(Puzzled)* What!? Jack can't have children, remember?

**EDNA:** It doesn't have to be with Jack.

**JILLY:** Mum! What're you suggesting!? That I go out and find another man, just to have his kids!?

**EDNA:** Yes.

**JILLY:** *(Aghast)* Do grandchildren mean that much to you?

**EDNA:** Yes, they do.

**JILLY:** And what about Jack?

**EDNA:** What about him?

**JILLY:** What's *he* going to say while I'm out picking up surrogate fathers?

**EDNA:** He doesn't have to know.

**JILLY:** He what..!? Don't you think he might be slightly suspicious if I suddenly announced I was pregnant?

**EDNA:** You'd find another man if Jack wasn't here.

**JILLY:** But he *is* here!

**EDNA:** But he might not *always* be here.

**JILLY:** *(After a pause to digest the meaning; agog)* What are you suggesting?

**EDNA:** Well... anything could happen. He could walk out of this flat tomorrow and get run over by a bus.

**JILLY:** Ugh! Don't be morbid.

**EDNA:** One of his more questionable clients might take it in mind to get even over some legal matter or other.

**JILLY:** You're mad!

**EDNA:** Anyway, let's face it, darling, you two aren't exactly the ideal picture of married bliss, are you?

**JILLY:** What d'you mean?

**EDNA:** You well know what I mean. When you're not arguing you're not speaking to each other!
**JILLY:** That's none of your business!
**EDNA:** You never know, you might even get divorced.
**JILLY:** There's no need to sound quite so keen on the idea.
**EDNA:** Well, it is possible.
**JILLY:** I don't believe I'm hearing this. A mother's supposed to *support* her daughter!
**EDNA:** Gillian, I *am* supporting you. Wouldn't you *like* children?
**JILLY:** Yes, of course I would, but...
**EDNA:** Then it's worth a thought.
**JILLY:** *(Standing; furious)* I am *not* divorcing Jack!
**EDNA:** Your children would have liked those trains.
**JILLY:** *(Obviously a sore point)* Enough, Mum! I don't want to talk about it.
**EDNA:** Still, it's not *your* fault, is it? *You* weren't to know when you married him.
**JILLY:** *(Sitting again)* No!

*(EDNA rises and moves up L. She runs her finger along the dust on the sideboard and looks at her finger in disgust.)*

**EDNA:** I still say, though, I always knew there was something peculiar about him. Something I couldn't put my finger on.
**JILLY:** He's not so bad, really... Or at least he wasn't.

*(JACK enters R with another case and some more carrier bags.)*

**JACK:** *(Moving L)* One of your carrier bags must have collapsed. *(He opens the door L and takes the luggage off. Off L)* There's blood all over the carpet in your car. *(He enters L and moves C.)* Looks like there's been a murder committed.
**EDNA:** Oh, damn. Must be from the steaks! Did you clear it up?
**JACK:** *(Indignant)* No..., I didn't!
**EDNA:** *(Assuming a pained expression)* But I can't do it with my back!

*(EDNA moves towards the settee and is about to sit.)*

**JACK:** Nor could I. Try a cloth. *(Seeing Edna about to sit; shouting)* Don't sit on that! *(He moves towards the settee.)*
**EDNA:** *(Standing bolt upright)* What!? Why not!? Whatever's wrong with it?
**JACK:** Nothing's wrong with it.... yet.
**EDNA:** Then what....?

## Wait Until The Ghost Is Clear

**JACK:** I've got to sleep on that later. If *you* sit there it'll be full of indentations and it'll stink of embrocation.

*(EDNA glares at him.)*

**JILLY:** *(Trying to defuse the argument)* Don't worry, Mum. I'll clean your car up later.

*(JACK gets his pistol and a cloth from the sideboard and starts to polish it as he moves up C.)*

**EDNA:** *(Moving up R)* Will you, darling? Thank you so much. At least *you* look after me.

**JACK:** *(To Edna)* I thought *you* were supposed to be looking after *her*.

**EDNA:** And so I shall. Someone has to. Some good food inside you, that's what you need, my girl. Good, *solid* food.

**JACK:** Like your sprouts, for example?

**EDNA:** And what is wrong with my sprouts?

**JACK:** Nothing at all... if you like eating sprouts through a straw.

**EDNA:** Oh, so we're going to insult my cooking now, are we?

**JACK:** "*We*"? Well, *I* was going to, but you can join in if you want.

**JILLY:** Now, Jack, don't start... You promised.

**EDNA:** Since when are you an authority on cooking, may one ask?

**JACK:** I'm not, but for God's sake, I was weaned onto solids when I was five.

**EDNA:** My cooking has won prizes.

**JACK:** Where!? Crufts!?

**JILLY:** *(Standing; tired of the arguments)* Will you two *please* stop bickering.

**EDNA:** Tell him to apologise.

**JILLY:** No!

**EDNA:** *(Taken aback by Jilly's response)* What?

**JACK:** She said, "No!"

**EDNA:** *(With umbrage)* So!? Now you're taking *his* side against me, are you?

**JACK:** *(Victorious)* Yes!

**JILLY:** *(Quickly)* No!

**JACK:** *(Surprised)* No?

**JILLY:** *(Firmly)* No! I'm not on anyone's side. *(She moves up R.)*

**EDNA:** But I'm your mother!

**JACK:** And *I'm* your husband.

**EDNA:** *(To Jack)* More's the pity.

## Wait Until The Ghost Is Clear

**JACK:** *(To Jilly)* Maybe, but that's how it is and *you* can't do anything about it!

**EDNA:** I know what I'd *like* to do!

**JACK:** *(Facing up to her)* What?

**JILLY:** *(Shouting and stamping her feet)* Stop it...! Stop it, stop it, stop it! *(When she has their attention she takes a step down C.)*

*(JACK and EDNA stop and look at her.)*

**EDNA:** Calm down, Gillian. Don't let him get to you. Remember, *I'm* here now. I'll protect you.

*(JACK shakes his head and sits on the settee. He starts to clean his gun. EDNA sits on the armchair. There is an uneasy silence for several seconds.)*

**JILLY:** Oh, that reminds me, Walter rang.

**JACK:** When?

**JILLY:** While you were getting Mum's bags.

**JACK:** What did he want?

**JILLY:** He wanted to know if you fancied going shooting tonight.

**JACK:** What did you tell him?

**JILLY:** I said you probably would.

**JACK:** What...!? *(Uneasy)* I... I can't go tonight. I've got work to do.

**JILLY:** Well he's going to pick you up at nine. You'd better phone him.

*(JACK checks his watch.)*

**JACK:** *(Standing)* Damn! *(He goes to the phone, dials and waits.)* Blast! No reply. He must have left.

**JILLY:** Phone him on his car phone.

**EDNA:** *(Muttering)* Car phones! Big kids!

*(JACK dials again and waits.)*

**JACK:** *(After a pause)* Still no reply! *(He slams down the phone.)*

**JILLY:** Well, you'll just have to tell him when he gets here, won't you?

**JACK:** Yes.... Damn! *(He is obviously troubled.)*

**JILLY:** What's the work, anyway?

**JACK:** *(Distracted)* Oh..., nothing. *(He sits on the settee.)*

**JILLY:** It must be a bit more than "nothing" to keep you away from the Gun Club.

**JACK:** No... No, it's nothing. Really.

**JILLY:** Is it money?

**JACK:** *(Reacting)* Of course it's money! It's *always* money! God knows where it all goes.

**JILLY:** *(Defensive)* Well, *I* don't spend it!

## Wait Until The Ghost Is Clear

**JACK:** You do your bit....! Anyway, I wasn't accusing you.
**JILLY:** Who, then?
**JACK:** Just forget it! I don't want to talk about it!
*(The uneasy silence returns.)*
**JILLY:** *(Moving C; trying to break the atmosphere)* So, Mum, how's Mrs Carter?
**EDNA:** *(To Jack)* Is that... thing loaded?
**JACK:** *(Cleaning)* No... *(He looks at Edna; with meaning)* More's the pity.
**JILLY:** Is she still working at the charity shop?
**EDNA:** *(Ignoring Jilly)* How exactly do you *know* it's not loaded?
**JACK:** Because I know. Because I'm used to handling guns.
**JILLY:** I went past there last week, and...
**EDNA:** But I'd like to know....
**JACK:** *(Suspicious)* What?
**JILLY:** *(Curious)* What?
**EDNA:** I said I should like to know... how you load it.
**JACK:** *(Pause)* This is a wind-up, isn't it?
**EDNA:** No it is not a "wind-up"! I mean it.
**JACK:** Really?
**EDNA:** Really.
**JACK:** *(He sits forward on the settee; a little hesitant)* Well, you pull this lever here and flip open the cylinder, then....
*(JACK looks at Edna and is surprised to find her apparently genuinely interested in his pistol. JILLY is amazed.)*
**JACK:** You take the bullets and put one in each of these chambers. Then, *(he is now totally engrossed in his hobby)* when it's full you close the cylinder. *(Demonstrating)* This is what they call a "double-action revolver", which means that the action of pressing the trigger cocks the hammer and also moves the cylinder round to line the next bullet up with the firing pin.
**EDNA:** I see.
**JACK:** But normally you leave it unloaded.
**EDNA:** Right. And how does one aim it?
**JACK:** *(Demonstrating)* Well, you line up the sight at the muzzle with the little notch here on the breech, see. *(He hands her the gun.)* Here, you try.
*(EDNA takes the pistol and follows instructions.)*
**JACK:** You have to get it dead centre, up-and-down and across. Then, when you're sure it's lined up exactly on target you squeeze the trigger.

## Wait Until The Ghost Is Clear

**EDNA:** Squeeze it?

**JACK:** Yes. If you pull it suddenly your aim goes.

**EDNA:** Can *I* try? It's not loaded?

**JACK:** No, all the ammunition's in the safe. *(He pats the settee beside him.)* Come and sit here and I'll show you.

*(EDNA rises and sits next to Jack. JACK takes the gun from her and demonstrates that it is empty. He hands it back to Edna. EDNA aims at a convenient ornament and pulls the trigger. It clicks.)*

**JACK:** *(Holding Edna's hands over the gun and steadying her)* Hold it more steady, like this. Now try.

*(EDNA pulls the trigger again. JACK lets her hands go and she aims at various objects and clicks the trigger, quite liking the feel of the gun.)*

**JACK:** That's it! You're a natural!

**EDNA:** *(Imitating Clint Eastwood, but in her posh accent)* Go on, punk... Make my day.

**JILLY:** I don't believe this! One minute you can't stand each other and the next you're like two lifelong mates.

**EDNA:** I was merely interested, that's all. You see these things on the television, but I've never actually seen one at close quarters before. *(She weighs the gun in her hand.)* Quite heavy, isn't it?

**JACK:** It's well-made.

*(The doorbell rings. JACK and EDNA are still looking at the gun. JILLY shakes her head and exits R. The door is heard to open off R.)*

**WALTER:** *(Off R)* Hello, Jilly.

**JILLY:** Walter!

**WALTER:** How's my favourite wife?

**JILLY:** *(Off R; squealing playfully)* Ouch! Walter! Don't do that!

*(JILLY enters R, rubbing her bottom, and moves down R. WALTER follows and moves C. He is a similar age to Jack, a merry man-about-town with an eye for the ladies. He is dressed in a trendy suit. As he enters he notices that EDNA has the gun pointing directly at him.)*

**WALTER:** *(Putting his hands up)* Don't shoot! I've a wife and six kids to support!

**JILLY:** No you haven't.

**WALTER:** No..., I haven't. *(He lowers his hands.)* O.K. fire away.

**JACK:** I was just showing Edna my pistol.

**WALTER:** So I see. Thinking of taking up shooting, Mum?

**EDNA:** No, just curious.

**WALTER:** Women can be very good at it, you know.

# Wait Until The Ghost Is Clear

**EDNA:** No, not me. *(She hands the gun back to Jack.)* Bridge is more *my* line.

**WALTER:** *(To Jack)* Ready, then?

**JACK:** *(Tense)* No. I tried to ring you. I can't come tonight.

**WALTER:** Can't come? You!? *(To Jilly)* Quick! Phone for an ambulance! *(He advances on Jack and feels his brow.)* O.K. tell the doctor all about it. How long have you been having these dizzy spells?

**JACK:** *(Pushing his hand away; irritated)* Don't mess about! I'm just tired, that's all.

**WALTER:** Tired!? You!?

**JILLY:** He's got some work to do, Walter.

**WALTER:** Work!? At this time of night!?

**JACK:** Yes... The er... The Johnson case.

**WALTER:** But that doesn't come to court for three weeks. Let it wait.

**JACK:** I can't. I've got to do some prep work.

**WALTER:** As your partner, I give you the night off. Now get your coat.

**JACK:** *(Firmly)* No, Walter! I've got to make a start.

**WALTER:** You'll end up with an ulcer.

**JACK:** *One* of us has to work!

**WALTER:** Ouch! I think I've just been reprimanded.

**JACK:** You know what I mean.

**WALTER:** You've got to have some time to yourself, Jack. give it a rest, eh?

**JACK:** *(Firm)* No!

**WALTER:** All right! I give in. *(He turns to Jilly.)* Tell you what, Jack!

**JACK:** What?

**WALTER:** If *you* won't come, I shall be forced to take your wife away from you. *(He grasps Jilly round the waist. Melodramatically)* Come, my dear! Let me take you away from all this!

**JILLY:** *(Not upset; struggling free)* Walter! Get off!

**WALTER:** Spurned! Rejected by those I love! Ah, me! I shall away and seek solace in the arms of the fair maidens of the Club bar. *(He moves to the door R. He turns.)* One last chance!

**JACK:** *(Impatient)* No!

**WALTER:** *(More serious)* This Johnson case must be serious.

**JACK:** It is!

**WALTER:** *(Moving towards Jack; concerned)* Are you *sure* that's all it is, Jack? You're behaving a bit odd.

**JACK:** *(Impatient)* Yes, yes, that's all. You go. I'll see you tomorrow.

**EDNA:** *(Standing)* Time I was going, too.
**JILLY:** I thought you were staying.
**EDNA:** I meant *going* to bed.
**JILLY:** What about dinner?
**EDNA:** Far too late for me, now. I shall make some cocoa and have a digestive. You'll have to get one of your Indian things.
**WALTER:** I know...! Edna, my love! Come with me to the Casbah!
**EDNA:** I'm *not* going to any bar with *you*. I am going to bed.
**WALTER:** Ah, well. At least I tried. *(He moves to the door R.)* Adieu...! *Adieu!*
**JILLY:** 'Bye, Walter. Close the door on your way out.
*(WALTER exits R. The front door is heard to open and close off R.)*
**JILLY:** *(Amused)* Walter's a right idiot!
**JACK:** *(Unimpressed)* Hilarious!
**JILLY:** You should have gone with him.
**JACK:** I told you, I've...
**JILLY:** *(Finishing for him)* ...got work to do!
**EDNA:** *(Moving to the door L)* Good night, Jack.
**JACK:** Good night, Edna.
**EDNA:** Good night. *(She exits L.)*
**JACK:** Leave the settee. I've got loads of work to do, so I doubt if I'll get much sleep anyway.
**JILLY:** *(Rising to the bait)* You're just trying to make me feel guilty.
**JACK:** *(Reacting)* So you should be! All this work to do and I can't even get a good night's sleep.
**JILLY:** Perhaps you should get a hotel room!
**JACK:** *(Shouting)* Don't tempt me!
**JILLY:** Shhh! Mother's in the other room!
**JACK:** I know! That's *why* I'm shouting, remember?
*(EDNA appears at the door L.)*
**EDNA:** Arguing again?
**JACK:** *(Sarcastic)* No! We're discussing knitting patterns.
**EDNA:** *(To Jack; accusing)* Did you bring my vanity case in?
**JACK:** *I* don't know. There was that much in your car I probably brought half the engine in. There was nothing left.
**EDNA:** I must have left it at home. My medicine was in it. I shall have to have it.
**JACK:** The Off-Licence is closer!

## Wait Until The Ghost Is Clear

**JILLY:** Jack!
**EDNA:** *(Moving to the door R)* I'll go and get it. I won't be long.
**JACK:** Take your time.

*(EDNA gives him a withering look and exits R. The front door is heard to open and close off R.)*

**JILLY:** You promised me you'd be nice to her.
**JACK:** I lied!

*(They sit in an uneasy silence for some moments. JACK finishes polishing his gun and puts it and the cloth on the table.)*

**JILLY:** I thought you had work to do.
**JACK:** I have. I'll do it in a minute. I'm not exactly looking forward to it.

*(There is a clattering noise off R.)*

**JILLY:** What was that?
**JACK:** Probably your mother come back to haunt us.
**JILLY:** *(Rising)* Mum...? Is that you?

*(Just as Jilly reaches the door R the lights black out completely. Almost immediately there is a single gunshot. Jilly screams.)*

**The CURTAIN falls.**

## ACT II

*A week later. Nine o'clock on the evening after Jack's funeral. As the curtain opens, JILLY is sitting alone on the armchair. She is dressed all in black. She has red eyes and has obviously been crying. She is controlled but still upset. SARAH, also in black, enters L carrying a tray with teapot, milk and two cups and saucers. JACK, dressed exactly as he was when he was shot, crouches behind the settee, unseen by the audience.)*

**SARAH:** *(Sympathetic)* Here, I've made us a cup of tea. *(She sees the bowl of peanuts in the centre of the table.)* Can you move the nuts?

**JILLY:** *(Moving the bowl of nuts to one side)* You know I can't bring myself to get rid of them.

**SARAH:** The nuts?

**JILLY:** Mmmm.. I can't stand the things, but Jack loved them. He was always chewing the damned things, it used to drive me crackers, and now he's gone I can't bring myself to throw them out.

**SARAH:** Then don't. Leave them there. *(She puts the tray down on the table.)* Here, have a cuppa. That'll help.

**JILLY:** God, what a day! *(She starts to sob again.)*

**SARAH:** *(Going to Jilly and comforting her)* I know, Jilly... But it's all over now. You can start rebuilding.

**JILLY:** *(Bitter)* If the Police'll let me.

**SARAH:** 'Course they will. You see.

**JILLY:** They think I killed him!

**SARAH:** No... They're just doing their job.

**JILLY:** *(Clutching at Sarah's arm)* I didn't Sarah! Really.... I didn't.

**SARAH:** *(Soothing)* I know you didn't. Just cast it out of your mind.

**JILLY:** You *do* believe me, don't you?

**SARAH:** Of course I believe you.

**JILLY:** Promise me! It's important *you* believe me... even if no-one else does.

**SARAH:** I *do* believe you. So does everyone else!

**JILLY:** They don't! That Police Inspector thinks I did it.

**SARAH:** Nonsense!

**JILLY:** And Walter.

**SARAH:** You're imagining things. Let me get you some tablets to help you sleep. You'll feel better in the morning.

**JILLY:** Even Mum thinks I did it.

**SARAH:** Of course she doesn't!

## Wait Until The Ghost Is Clear

**JILLY:** She does! She's not even speaking to me.
**SARAH:** What?
**JILLY:** We had a row... She walked out. *(Tearful)* How could she..!? My own mother!
**SARAH:** *(Crouching before her and taking both hands in hers)* Jilly! Snap out of it! Nobody thinks you killed Jack. Why should they? Why should *you*?
**JILLY:** As long as *you* believe me.
**SARAH:** I told you....
**JILLY:** I know we had our ups and downs... more downs than ups lately, but I'd never....
**SARAH:** *(Standing)* I'll get those tablets.
**JILLY:** *(Reluctant to let go)* No! Don't leave me!
**SARAH:** I'm only going to the kitchen. I'll be back before you know it.
*(SARAH rises and moves to the door L. Before she reaches it the doorbell rings off R.)*
**JILLY:** *(Starting)* Who's that!?
**SARAH:** You sit down. I'll go.
*(SARAH exits R. JILLY looks uneasily about the room. The door is heard to open off R.)*
**JAMES:** *(Off R)* Good evening, Miss Watts. Is Mrs Hardy at home?
**SARAH:** *(Off R; annoyed)* Oh, I don't believe it! Don't you ever let up?
**JAMES:** *(After a pause; businesslike)* Well, Miss?
**SARAH:** *(After a pause; resigned)* In there.
*(INSPECTOR JAMES enters R. She carries a few cardboard folders - which she is almost dropping - and looks generally dishevelled and bumbling. SARAH follows.)*
**JAMES:** Good evening, Mrs Hardy. I wonder if I might trouble you for a few minutes?
**JILLY:** *(Nervous)* What is it? What d'you want now? I've told you all I know hundreds of times already.
**JAMES:** Just one or two small details, if you don't mind. *(Pause)* May I sit? *(Without waiting for a reply, she sits on the settee and searches through her folders until she finds the one she is looking for. She puts the rest in an untidy heap beside her. She reaches in her bag, takes out a notebook and rummages around for a pen.)*
**SARAH:** *(Forcing herself to be polite)* Would you like some tea, Inspector?
**JAMES:** *(Still searching)* Yes... That would be nice, Miss. Er... you wouldn't have a pen I could borrow?
**JILLY:** *(Flustered)* Er...

**SARAH:** *(Taking a pen from next to the telephone and thrusting it at Inspector James)* Here!

**JAMES:** *(Taking the pen)* Ah... Thank you.

**SARAH:** Will you be alright, Jilly?

**JILLY:** Yes... Yes, go on.

*(SARAH casts a doubtful glance at the pair and exits L.)*

**JAMES:** *(Opening the folder)* Now, Mrs Hardy.... Your husband....

**JILLY:** What about him?

**JAMES:** Your husband left a will, I believe?

**JILLY:** Yes.

**JAMES:** And in that will, apart from his interest in the business, which he left to his partner, a Mr *(consulting her file)* Walter Stern, he left everything to you. Is that correct?

**JILLY:** I think you know it's not.

**JAMES:** Ah, yes, the little matter of the legacy to your mother. You knew about that, of course?

**JILLY:** No. Nothing. I should have though she was the last person he'd leave a penny to...

**JAMES:** They didn't get on with one another?

**JILLY:** I *thought* he hated her.

**JAMES:** *(Making notes)* And your mother... Did she hate *him*?

**JILLY:** *(Suddenly suspicious)* What are you trying to say?

**JAMES:** Nothing, Mrs Hardy, nothing.... Just exploring all avenues.

**JILLY:** *(Defensive) My* mother....

**JAMES:** *(Interrupting)* Did he have any life insurance policies?

**JILLY:** *(Annoyed)* You know he did. You took them away, remember?

**JAMES:** Yes. Quite so. A total of twenty-two thousand pounds, wasn't it?

**JILLY:** Yes.

**JAMES:** Not a bad sum. But hardly enough to live on, eh? *(After a pause; suspicious)* What about his safe deposit box?

**JILLY:** *(After a pause; puzzled) What* safe deposit box?

*(SARAH enters L.)*

**JAMES:** *(To Sarah; curt)* Could you wait outside, please, Miss?

**JILLY:** *(Angry)* No, she couldn't! Come in, Sarah.

**JAMES:** But I'd rather speak to you alone...

**JILLY:** I don't care *what* you'd rather do, Inspector. You've been on my back since the day Jack *(she pauses - the word is difficult to say)* died. And I've had enough of it. So if *I* want Sarah here then you'll damned-well have to

## Wait Until The Ghost Is Clear

put up with it!

**JAMES:** *(After a pause; with controlled anger)* Very well, Mrs Hardy.

*(SARAH brings in the spare cup. Over the next few lines she pours the tea and hands it round.)*

**JAMES:** Now, as I was saying, Mrs Hardy, did you know about his safe deposit box?

**JILLY:** And as *I* was saying, Inspector, *what* safe deposit box?

**JAMES:** I take it you didn't know he had one, then.

**JILLY:** *(A glance at Sarah)* No, Inspector. I didn't.

**JAMES:** Don't you find it odd that he didn't tell you about it?

**JILLY:** Er... no... Not really. He never told me much about the business.

**JAMES:** Did he have *many* secrets from you, Mrs Hardy?

**SARAH:** Inspector James! Can't you leave her alone? She buried her husband today.

**JAMES:** *(Calm; to Sarah)* I am well aware of that, Miss Watts... *(Turning to Jilly)* Please answer the question, Mrs Hardy.

**JILLY:** *(Frosty)* None that I know of.

**JAMES:** I see.

**JILLY:** But, then again, if I *knew* about them, they wouldn't be secrets, would they?

**JAMES:** No.., quite. *(She drinks her tea.)*

**JILLY:** *(Unable to contain her curiosity)* Er... this safe deposit box... What was in it?

**JAMES:** Various things, Mrs Hardy. Some business papers, some letters.... *(She pauses.)*

**JILLY:** *(Realising there must be more)* And...?

**JAMES:** And *another* life insurance policy.

**JILLY:** Another one!?

**JAMES:** Yes... It seems you're a very rich widow, Mrs Hardy.

**JILLY:** *(Puzzled)* What?

**JAMES:** It seems he was insured for just over three hundred thousand pounds.

*(JILLY is speechless. She and SARAH stare at each other open-mouthed.)*

**SARAH:** *(After a pause)* Three hundred thousand!? You're joking!

**JAMES:** Hardly a matter for levity, Miss.

**SARAH:** Why, the old....

**JILLY:** Why would he do that?

**JAMES:** The very question that's been puzzling us, Mrs Hardy. Why should a man of forty-two with a thriving law partnership take out a life insurance policy for over a quarter of a million pounds? Have you any idea?

**JILLY:** *(Still stunned; shaking her head)* No.

**JAMES:** *(With effect)* What's more, why should he do it *two days* before he is murdered?

**SARAH:** What!?

**JAMES:** That's right, Miss. Two days.

**JILLY:** I don't believe it.

**JAMES:** I'm afraid it's true, Mrs Hardy. *(Searching through her other folders)* I have a copy here somewhere. *(She finds the one she is looking for, opens it and shows it to Jilly)* So I'm sure you can appreciate why we're suspicious.

**JILLY:** *(Looking in amazement at the folder)* Yes, but...... *(Realising)* Wait a minute! You think that I...!

**JAMES:** We don't think anything, Mrs Hardy. Not yet.

**JILLY:** I never knew about it, I tell you..! Oh, my God!

**JAMES:** Was yours a *happy* marriage, Mrs Hardy?

**SARAH:** What sort of question's that!?

**JAMES:** *(Insistent)* Was it?

**SARAH:** Of course it was!

**JAMES:** *(Frosty)* I'd like Mrs Hardy to answer, if you don't mind, Miss. *(JILLY is speechless.)*

**JAMES:** Well?

**JILLY:** I... I... Yes...! Well, we had our arguments, of course, but every married couple... I mean.... everyone argues now and again, don't they?

**JAMES:** Do they, Mrs Hardy?

**SARAH:** *(To the Inspector)* I think you'd better leave!

**JAMES:** *(Gathering her papers together)* Yes, Miss. Perhaps you're right. I'll see you tomorrow. *(She finishes her tea. Unfeeling)* But, as they say on television, don't leave town, will you?

**SARAH:** *(Enraged)* Go!

**JAMES:** *(Standing and moving to the door R)* Very well. *(She stops at the door.)* Oh... One more question.

**SARAH:** What now!?

**JAMES:** Your husband's pistol. Did he look after it? Keep it well cleaned, and so on?

**JILLY:** Yes. He was always messing about with it. *(Without thinking)* Sometimes I think he thought more of that gun than.... *(She stops herself.)*

**JAMES:** Than *you*, Mrs Hardy?

## Wait Until The Ghost Is Clear

**JILLY:** A figure of speech, Inspector.

**JAMES:** Hmmm... I'll see myself out. Goodnight, ladies.

*(The INSPECTOR exits R, and the door is heard to open and shut. SARAH and JILLY look at each other in disbelief.)*

**JILLY:** I *told* you! I said she...

*(SARAH puts her finger to her lips to silence Jilly. She exits R, watched by Jilly, then returns.)*

**SARAH:** She's gone. You never know...

**JILLY:** She thinks *I* did it!

**SARAH:** So what if she does? She doesn't *know* anything! She's just guessing.

**JILLY:** I tell you she thinks I did it. It was bad enough before, but now...

**SARAH:** *(Dreamy)* Three hundred thousand...!

**JILLY:** *(Glum)* The perfect motive!

**SARAH:** Yes.... *Too* perfect!

**JILLY:** What d'you mean?

**SARAH:** It's a bit of a coincidence, isn't it? Jack takes out an insurance policy for a small fortune, then two days later he conveniently gets shot with his own gun.

**JILLY:** *(Near to tears)* And everything points to me!

**SARAH:** Like I said, too much of a coincidence.

**JILLY:** Sarah! What am I going to do?

**SARAH:** There's no proof, Jilly!

**JILLY:** God, you sound like a defence lawyer!

**SARAH:** Assuming you didn't kill him.... *(A pause.)* Jilly, forgive me, but I have to ask....

**JILLY:** *(Misunderstanding; hurt)* Sarah! *(She calms herself. Through gritted teeth)* No! I didn't! How could you!?

**SARAH:** I didn't mean...! My God, Jilly, *that* wasn't what I was going to ask. What d'you think I am!?

**JILLY:** You said you believed me!

**SARAH:** *(Quickly)* I do, I do! You must know that.

**JILLY:** *(Eventually; calming herself)* Alright, I believe you.

**SARAH:** *(Sitting on the R end of the settee)* I was going to ask you if you and Walter ever....? *(She trails off.)*

**JILLY:** *(Shocked)* Sarah!

**SARAH:** Well, it's obvious he fancies you.

**JILLY:** *(Firmly)* It is not.... *(Dubious)* Is it?

**SARAH:** Very.

**JILLY:** *(Shocked)* God, I never realised... *(She shakes her head in disbelief.)* Anyway... No we didn't.

**SARAH:** Right! Let's examine the evidence. Jack had a huge insurance policy. He was shot with his own gun, in this room.

**JILLY:** Alone, with me... Sarah, I'm the *only* suspect.

**SARAH:** But it wasn't you.

**JILLY:** Try telling Inspector James that!

**SARAH:** So we have to find out who it *was*.

**JILLY:** How?

**SARAH:** Who had a motive to kill Jack?

**JILLY:** Nobody. Everybody loved him.

**SARAH:** Except you...

**JILLY:** Oh, thanks! Right back to *me* again. Anyway, I *did* love him... In my own way.

**SARAH:** ...And your mother.

**JILLY:** Jilly! What are you saying!?

**SARAH:** Well, she didn't, did she?

**JILLY:** No, but I refuse to believe that Mum...

**SARAH:** We have to consider everything. What about Walter?

**JILLY:** What about him?

**SARAH:** Could *he* have done it?

**JILLY:** *(Immediately)* No, of course not!

**SARAH:** Sure?

**JILLY:** Yes...! I mean... why would he? He had nothing to gain, and everything to lose.

**SARAH:** What about the business?

**JILLY:** What about it?

**SARAH:** Would he benefit from Jack's death?

**JILLY:** Well, he gets the rest of the business, if that's what you mean, but...

**SARAH:** Ah! A motive!

**JILLY:** ...but he'll not do very well without Jack.

**SARAH:** Why not?

**JILLY:** Jack was the brains of the outfit. If Walter said that once he said it a hundred times. "Jack," he'd say, "I'm hopeless! If it wasn't for you we'd go bust!"

**SARAH:** Jealousy, then.

## Wait Until The Ghost Is Clear

**JILLY:** No. They were the best of mates.

**SARAH:** He had the weapon, and he knew how to use it.

**JILLY:** Jack's gun?

**SARAH:** No... his *own* gun. Don't you see...? They were identical, weren't they?

**JILLY:** So? It was *Jack's* gun that did the shooting. The Police said.

**SARAH:** Why couldn't it have been *Walter's* gun? If they're identical maybe you can't tell the difference.

**JILLY:** You're clutching at straws, now. The Police examined the gun. It was Jack's, and it had been fired. They checked Walter's too. They checked the serial numbers. *And* they did a ballistics check.

**SARAH:** I still think it's a bit suspicious.

**JILLY:** You've got an evil mind.

**SARAH:** Maybe, but be realistic... someone did it. Were there any fingerprints on the gun?

**JILLY:** I don't know... They never told me. *(Pause)* Maybe it was an accident. Perhaps Jack left the gun loaded and it went off. It was dark, remember.

**SARAH:** *(Dubious)* Hmmm... Maybe.

**JILLY:** Perhaps someone loaded the gun in the hope it would go off.

**SARAH:** That's a hell of a coincidence. And surely Jack would have noticed. He was always so careful.

*(They are silent for some moments.)*

**JILLY:** It's hopeless, isn't it?

**SARAH:** Never say die! *(Realising what she has said)* Sorry. Slip of the tongue.

**JILLY:** Apology accepted.

**SARAH:** How about if we recreate the scene of the crime, like they do on that Police programme? It might trigger you to remember something.

**JILLY:** You've been watching too much television!

**SARAH:** It's worth a try.... Come on. It's better than sitting here feeling sorry for ourselves.

**JILLY:** *(Resigned)* Very well.... What d'you want me to do?

**SARAH:** Where were you... just before...?

**JILLY:** Sitting here. I always sit here.

**SARAH:** Where was Jack?

**JILLY:** On the settee.

**SARAH:** Where I am?

**JILLY:** No. The other end.

SARAH: What were you doing?
JILLY: Talking.
SARAH: What about?
JILLY: *(Impatient)* I can't remember. Probably arguing about my mother staying, knowing us.
SARAH: Then what happened?
JILLY: There was a noise in the hall.
SARAH: What sort of noise?
JILLY: I don't know. Just a noise. A banging noise.
SARAH: Footsteps?
JILLY: Could have been. It sounded more like the door.
SARAH: It could have been the murderer!
*(JILLY shudders.)*
SARAH: What did you do?
JILLY: Jack said something about it being Mum coming back to haunt us.
SARAH: Then what happened?
JILLY: I got up and went to the door.
SARAH: *(Indicating for her to do so)* Go on then.
JILLY: What?
SARAH: Do it. Like you did then.
*(JILLY looks uneasily at Sarah, rises and goes to the door R.)*
JILLY: I said "Mum...? Is that you?" and the lights went out, like this... *(She reaches out and switches off the light.)*
SARAH: You *switched* them off?
JILLY: No. They just went off on their own. Then there was a shot. I think I screamed. Then the lights came on again and...
*(JILLY switches the lights on again, still facing the door. As the lights snap on, JACK is sitting next to Sarah on the settee. SARAH does not see him.)*
JILLY: ....when I turned round and my eyes became accustomed to the light, Jack was *(She sees Jack. Her hand flies to her mouth in horror.)* Oh, my God!
JACK: *(His old self; starting and looking up)* Jilly! Don't do that!
SARAH: *(Starting)* What is it?
*(JILLY stares, speechless.)*
JACK: *(Starting; suddenly noticing Sarah)* Sarah! How did you get here?
SARAH: *(Standing and going to Jilly)* Jilly! Tell me! What's wrong!?
*(JILLY looks from Jack to Sarah in total shock and then back to Jack.)*
JILLY: Jack!

## Wait Until The Ghost Is Clear

JACK: *(Matter-of-fact)* What?
SARAH: *(Puzzled)* What!?
JILLY: *(Suddenly noticing Sarah)* Jack!
SARAH: What about him?
JACK: Yes, what about me?

*(JILLY is moving her lips but is speechless. She can only point. SARAH looks at Jack, but sees nothing.)*

SARAH: That's where he was?

*(JILLY nods, speechless.)*

SARAH: I'm sorry, Jilly. I didn't mean to bring it all back. Come and sit down.

*(SARAH tries to lead JILLY back to her armchair, but JILLY resists, staring at Jack.)*

JILLY: But... he's here. I can see him.

*(SARAH manages to sit her down.)*

SARAH: *(Calming)* It's only natural you should feel like that. It's only two weeks since he went.

JILLY: And now he's back!

*(SARAH sits on the settee in front of the tea tray and tests to see how much is in the pot.)*

JACK: Jilly, what *are* you going on about?
JILLY: *(To Jack)* What're you doing?
JACK: Nothing. Just sitting here. Why?
SARAH: Getting you another cup of tea. Calm you down.
JACK: *(To Jilly)* Is there enough for me?
SARAH: Damn, empty!
JILLY: *(To Jack)* How can you just sit there?
JACK: It's all right. Sarah doesn't mind, do you, Sarah?
SARAH: *(Surprised at Jilly's attitude)* O.K., O.K... I'll go and make some more.
JILLY: *(Hearing Sarah at last)* No! Don't leave me!
SARAH: *(Calming)* It's all right! I won't be a minute.
JILLY: *(Desperate)* Sarah!

*(SARAH picks up the teapot and exits L. JILLY still stares at JACK in disbelief.)*

JILLY: I must be dreaming.
JACK: What's that?
JILLY: *(Without thinking)* I said, "I must be dreaming".

39

## Wait Until The Ghost Is Clear

| | |
|---|---|
| **JACK:** | What about? |
| **JILLY:** | I don't believe this. I'm talking to myself. |
| **JACK:** | First sign of madness, that. |
| **JILLY:** | It *is* you, isn't it? |
| **JACK:** | What is? |
| **JILLY:** | Sitting there. |
| **JACK:** | Jilly, have you been at your mother's gin? |
| **JILLY:** | Now I *know* it's you. |
| **JACK:** | *(Humouring her)* Yes... If you say so. |
| **JILLY:** | But it can't be. |
| **JACK:** | No. Probably not. |
| **JILLY:** | *(Rising)* I don't believe this! I'm going mad. |

*(JILLY crosses to the light switch and turns off the lights.)*

| | |
|---|---|
| **JACK:** | Oi! Turn those lights on! |

*(JILLY turns the lights back on. JACK is still there. JILLY goes to him.)*

| | |
|---|---|
| **JILLY:** | *(Ashen)* It *is* you! |
| **JACK:** | *(Losing patience)* Jilly, what *is* the matter with you? You look as if you've seen a ghost. |
| **JILLY:** | I think I have. |
| **JACK:** | Very funny. |
| **JILLY:** | I mean it, Jack. |
| **JACK:** | *(Noticing she is serious)* You're serious, aren't you? |
| **JILLY:** | Deadly...! Er... very! |
| **JACK:** | *(Looking round)* What did you see...? Where!? |
| **JILLY:** | You...! Here...! |
| **JACK:** | Jilly, what....? |
| **JILLY:** | Jack... you don't know, do you? |
| **JACK:** | *(Puzzled)* Know what? |
| **JILLY:** | D'you know where I was earlier today? |
| **JACK:** | Er, let me think. *(He thinks for a moment.)* Out shopping with the dragon. |
| **JILLY:** | You don't know what day it is, do you? |
| **JACK:** | 'Course I do. It's Wednesday. |
| **JILLY:** | Monday. |
| **JACK:** | Don't be stupid, Jilly. |
| **JILLY:** | Jack, it's Monday. |
| **JACK:** | You *have* been drinking, haven't you? |

## Wait Until The Ghost Is Clear

**JILLY:** *(Rising)* I'll prove it to you.
*(JILLY fetches the newspaper from the table. She shows it to Jack.)*
**JILLY:** There!
**JACK:** The newspaper! What about it?
**JILLY:** Look at the date.
**JACK:** *(Looking at the paper to humour her)* Jilly, I don't know what you.... *(He notices the date.)* But.... That's impossible!
**JILLY:** Monday the twenty-third!
**JACK:** But how....? What...? Have I been asleep for two weeks?
**JILLY:** Look here... *(She turns to the page)* Page seventeen.
**JACK:** *(Looking; puzzled)* Well...?
**JILLY:** Down at the bottom.
**JACK:** *(Puzzled)* What...? Jilly, I.... *(He notices. His eyes widen in shock.)* Oh, my God...! *(He reads)* "...The funeral of Jack William Hardy, beloved husband of Gillian...!"
*(JACK looks at Jilly and then back at the paper several times in total disbelief.)*
**JACK:** You mean I'm....? That's...... me!?
**JILLY:** Exactly!
**JACK:** *(Shocked)* I must be dreaming.
**JILLY:** One of us must!
**JACK:** Dead!? Me!?
**JILLY:** Either that or I've gone mad and I'm imagining you.
**JACK:** But I can't be dead! I'm sitting here! You're talking to me!
**JILLY:** You were shot. Right here.
**JACK:** Was I?
**JILLY:** Yes.
**JACK:** Shot!?
**JILLY:** With your own gun.
**JACK:** *(After a pause)* Perhaps I got better.
**JILLY:** Sorry, Jack. I was at your funeral. The grieving widow!
**JACK:** I thought you'd be glad to see the back of me!
**JILLY:** So did I! *(She shakes her head rapidly in disbelief.)* I still can't believe this!
**JACK:** Shot, you say?
**JILLY:** Right through the chest.
*(JACK pulls the neck of his shirt out and looks down for wounds.)*

## Wait Until The Ghost Is Clear

**JACK:** Looks O.K.... Dead...!?

*(They stare at each other in a silence of disbelief.)*

**JACK:** *(Thinking he has been taken for a ride)* This is a joke, isn't it? A wind-up?

**JILLY:** Jack! This is serious!

**JACK:** Very good, Jilly. You had me going for a minute, there.

**JILLY:** Jack...!

*(SARAH enters R carrying the teapot.)*

**JACK:** *(His back to Sarah)* That phoney newspaper's very good. Where did you get it done? *(He notices Sarah.)* Ah, Sarah, are you in on the joke, too?

**SARAH:** *(Pouring the tea)* Here we are. This'll make you feel better.

**JACK:** *(Admiring the way she is "ignoring" him)* Very good, Sarah! You should have been an actress. But you can stop it, now. I've got it sussed. Had me fooled for a minute or two, but....

*(SARAH finishes pouring Jilly's tea, which she gives her.)*

**JACK:** *(To Sarah)* Didn't you bring me one?

**SARAH:** *(Moving L)* I'll get you those tablets. They'll help you sleep.

**JILLY:** *(Weakly)* Thanks.

**JACK:** Oh, come on, you two... A joke's a joke, but this isn't funny any more.

*(SARAH exits L.)*

**JILLY:** It's not a joke, Jack. It's serious. *Dead*ly serious.

**JACK:** *(Still not believing)* Rubbish! I don't believe in ghosts. Nor do you.

**JILLY:** No.... I *didn't*.

**JACK:** Come on, give it up now. You're making me nervous.

*(JILLY retains her serious, worried expression.)*

**JACK:** O.K., if *you* won't give in, I'll make Sarah. I can always make Sarah laugh.

**JILLY:** *(After a sigh)* Go ahead. Try your luck.

*(SARAH enters L carrying a glass of water and two tablets. As she enters, JACK makes faces at her. She does not see him.)*

**SARAH:** Here you are. Take these. *(She hands the water and tablets to Jilly, then resumes her place on the settee.)*

*(JACK waves his hands in front of her eyes, but she takes no notice.)*

**JILLY:** *(Putting the water and tablets down)* I don't want them, Sarah. I don't want to sleep. Jack... *(She trails off.)*

## Wait Until The Ghost Is Clear

**SARAH:** It'll all seem clearer in the morning.
**JACK:** *(To Sarah; puckering his lips)* Give us a kiss.
**SARAH:** A good night's sleep'll do you the world of good.
**JACK:** Go on! You know I've always fancied you, Sarah.
**JILLY:** Sarah, I can't....
**SARAH:** You're bound to be tense after the funeral.
**JACK:** "Funeral"! Very good, Sarah.
*(SARAH finishes her tea and sits back on the settee.)*
**JILLY:** *(Hopelessly)* I can't! You don't understand. Jack...
**SARAH:** I know, Jilly....
*(JACK sits on Sarah's knee and puts his arms round her neck. She notices nothing and carries on as normal. He toys with her hair.)*
**SARAH:** Shall I call the Doctor?
**JILLY:** Jack! Get off!
**SARAH:** *(Deciding on a firmer approach)* Now, Jilly, this has gone far enough. You're being irrational!
**JILLY:** *(As calm as she is able)* Sarah, I know you don't believe me, but Jack is *here...*, *now....*, in this room.
**SARAH:** *(After a pause)* You're right. I don't believe you.
**JILLY:** For God's sake, Sarah! He's sitting on your knee.
**SARAH:** *(Sarcastic)* Oh, yes, Jilly. I can see him.
**JILLY:** *(With hope)* You can?
**SARAH:** Yes. Here he is. *(To an imaginary Jack)* Why, Jack, I never knew you cared!
**JILLY:** Oh, I do, Sarah. I always have.
**SARAH:** And what a curious pink suit you're wearing. And those yellow shoes! Perfect!
**JILLY:** *(Deflated)* Now you're making fun.
**SARAH:** Well... What d'you expect?
**JILLY:** I expect you to believe me!
*(SARAH stands as if Jack is not there and tips him on the floor.)*
**JACK:** Ow! *(He picks himself up and sits on the settee.)*
**SARAH:** Jilly. Listen to me... *(She crouches before Jilly and takes her hands in her own)* It's been a long, hard day. You're tired. It's quite natural for you to miss Jack.
**JILLY:** I *don't* miss him...! *Didn't!*
**JACK:** Oh, *very* nice! Some sort of widow *you* turned out to be! Now look, Jilly....

43

## Wait Until The Ghost Is Clear

**SARAH:** But you've got to snap out of this.
**JACK:** Stay out of this, Sarah! I'll sort her out. Jilly, once and for all...
**JILLY:** *(Appealing)* Sarah...! Jack...!
**SARAH:** Shall I call your Mum?
**JACK:** *(Quickly)* No!
**JILLY:** *(Firm)* No, Sarah!
**SARAH:** Then you must get a grip on yourself.
**JACK:** Yes, Jilly. Get a grip on yourself! *(Moving to her as if he is going to strangle her)* Before *I* do!
**JILLY:** *(Calm)* I've *got* a grip on myself. My head is clear, I feel perfectly rational and calm.... but....

*(JACK and SARAH are now standing side by side in front of Jilly.)*

**SARAH:** But what?
**JILLY:** *(Losing all semblance of calm)* But Jack is standing here next to us!
**SARAH:** *(Losing her cool)* Oh, I give up!
**JILLY:** *(Pleading; in the general direction of both of them)* Please... You've got to help me.
**SARAH:** *(Taking a deep breath)* What?
**JACK:** Why should I?
**JILLY:** You're my best friend, yes?
**SARAH:** Yes.
**JACK:** Huh!
**JILLY:** And have I ever lied to you?
**JACK:** All the time.
**SARAH:** Not that I know of.
**JILLY:** Have you ever known me be irrational or imagine things?
**JACK:** Yes. Often.
**SARAH:** Not before today.
**JILLY:** Then why won't you believe me?
**JACK:** Because this is stupid! I mean, a joke's a joke, but this has gone too far... *(He looks to both women waiting for them to give in, then turns away when they do not.)*
**SARAH:** *(Deciding the best approach)* All right. I believe you.
**JILLY:** *(Hopeful)* You do?
**SARAH:** Yes... I believe *you* believe Jack is here.
**JILLY:** *(Deflated)* In other words you don't.
**SARAH:** I didn't say that.

## Wait Until The Ghost Is Clear

**JILLY:** But that's what you mean.

**SARAH:** No, it's not. Like I said before, you've had a difficult time over the past couple of weeks, what with settling all Jack's affairs and so on...

**JACK:** What affaires? I never had any affaires!

**SARAH:** And today has probably been the breaking point. Your mind's playing tricks on you. You really believe Jack *is* here.... But, be honest with yourself... He can't be, can he...? You saw the body. You saw him cremated....

**JACK:** *(Concerned)* Cremated!? That's a bit final, isn't it?

**SARAH:** I'm right, aren't I?

**JILLY:** *(After consideration)* Yes, I suppose so.

**SARAH:** That's it.

**JILLY:** I think I must be going mad.

**SARAH:** No you're not! It's just a temporary aberration.

**JILLY:** You think so?

**SARAH:** I *know* so.

**JILLY:** *(Looking directly at Jack)* So Jack isn't really here at all?

**SARAH:** No.

**JILLY:** I can still see him.

**SARAH:** You still want me to stay tonight?

**JILLY:** Oh, yes. Please. I don't want to be alone.

**SARAH:** Right. You sit there and drink that tea. I'll go and make up the bed.

**JILLY:** *(Starting to stand)* No, I can do it.

**SARAH:** *(Firmly)* No you can't! *I'll* do it.

**JILLY:** *(Sitting again)* Very well.

*(SARAH casts a worried look at Jilly and exits L. JACK wanders round the room with slight concern while JILLY watches. Eventually he advances to her.)*

**JACK:** Are you going to stop this rubbish or not?

**JILLY:** I'm not listening to you. You're not here!

**JACK:** *(Angry)* Oh, for God's sake, Jilly...!

**JILLY:** You're a figment!

**JACK:** *(Enraged)* A figment!?

**JILLY:** Yes, a figment! Of *my* troubled imagination!

**JACK:** Or a ghost.

**JILLY:** Is there a difference?

**JACK:** But it's ridiculous... If I was a ghost I could.... I could walk through that wall.

# Wait Until The Ghost Is Clear

**JILLY:** How d'you know ghosts can really do that sort of thing? Have you ever met one?

**JACK:** No... but in all the stories they can. Perhaps I should try.

*(JACK stands, takes a deep breath and walks at the wall. He bounces off and nurses his bruises.)*

**JACK:** That wasn't very ghostly, was it? That felt very lifelike.

**JILLY:** *(Firm)* You're a figment, Jack! *(Bitter)* Couldn't you be satisfied with making my life a misery when you were alive... D'you have to do it after you're dead as well!

**JACK:** I'll show you how much of a figment I am.

*(JACK grasps Jilly's wrist. JILLY sees him grasp her and pulls easily away. He takes her wrist again and she looks at his grip on her but does not move.)*

**JILLY:** *(Pleased with herself)* Hah! That proves it!

**JACK:** What proves what?

**JILLY:** I can't feel you.

**JACK:** What!?

**JILLY:** You heard.

**JACK:** *(Troubled now)* I can feel *you*. *(After a pause)* You can't feel anything?

**JILLY:** Not a thing.

**JACK:** *("Squeezing" harder)* Can you feel that?

**JILLY:** No.

*(JACK "squeezes" really hard until finally he has to break the grip. JILLY has not felt a thing. JACK flexes his fingers, then examines her unmarked wrist.)*

**JACK:** *(Really concerned)* Not a mark.

**JILLY:** Like I said. You're a figment. *(She picks up the bowl of peanuts and offers them to him.)* Have a peanut. You know you love them.

**JACK:** *(Absentmindedly reaching for the nuts)* Thanks. *(He tries to pick up some nuts but cannot. He looks amazed at his hand.)* That's stupid. I can *feel* them.

**JILLY:** *(Victorious)* But you *can't* pick them up, can you?

**JACK:** *(Defeated; sitting on the settee)* Then it's true.... *(After a pause)* I don't *feel* like a figment.

**JILLY:** Well, you are... Sorry.

**JACK:** *Sorry*!? Is that all you can say?

**JILLY:** What am I *supposed* to say?

**JACK:** You could be a bit more sympathetic.

**JILLY:** To a figment?
**JACK:** If I *am* a figment, does that mean I'll go away?
**JILLY:** Probably. How should I know? I've never had a figment before.
**JACK:** *(Fed up)* I suppose I'd better just wait here until I disappear, then.
**JILLY:** Yes.

*(They sit in silence, looking around as if expecting something to happen.)*

**JACK:** I wish I could have a nut.

*(JILLY glares at him. They resume the silence. JACK twiddles his thumbs.)*

**JACK:** Nothing's happening.
**JILLY:** No. Nor me.

*(They sit in silence again.)*

**JACK:** Jilly.
**JILLY:** What?
**JACK:** While I'm waiting for me to disappear, can we talk?
**JILLY:** Suppose so. What d'you want to talk about?
**JACK:** Well, for a start... who killed me?
**JILLY:** *I* don't know. Do you?
**JACK:** It wasn't you, then?
**JILLY:** *(Offended)* No! How dare you!?
**JACK:** Just asking. Then again I don't suppose you'd tell me if you did.
**JILLY:** Why not? You're hardly likely to tell anyone else, are you?
**JACK:** No. *(A pause.)* Was it your mother?
**JILLY:** What?
**JACK:** Who killed me?
**JILLY:** *(Indignant)* No!
**JACK:** Are you sure?
**JILLY:** Yes, I am! The very idea!
**JACK:** She might have done. She never liked me.
**JILLY:** You never gave her any reason to like you, did you?
**JACK:** And she was *very* interested in my pistol.
**JILLY:** So what? She was just being nice.
**JACK:** Very out of character.

*(SARAH enters L.)*

**SARAH:** Right. The bed's all made up. Come on.
**JILLY:** He's still here.
**SARAH:** Don't worry. He'll go. Now come to bed.
**JACK:** Can I come with you?

**JILLY:** No!
**SARAH:** What!?
**JILLY:** It was Jack. He said he wants to come to bed with me.
**SARAH:** Ignore him. He's not really there, remember?
**JILLY:** I am *not* having Jack coming up to bed with me... us!
**SARAH:** Why not?
**JACK:** Yes, Jilly. Why not?
**JILLY:** *(To Sarah)* Not while *you're* here.
**SARAH:** *I* don't mind.
**JACK:** Nor do I.
**JILLY:** *I* do.
**SARAH:** I give up. Come to bed when you're finished arguing with.... Jack. *(She exits L.)*
**JACK:** Hah! You're afraid of sleeping with a ghost.
**JILLY:** No, it's not that. After all, before you were killed it was a bit like sleeping with a corpse!
**JACK:** *(Indignant)* What!?
**JILLY:** You were hardly very active, were you? But it's not that. It's Sarah.
**JACK:** *(Indignant)* Sleeping in *my* bed?
**JILLY:** Yes.
**JACK:** *(Starting L; rubbing his hands in glee)* I can't wait!
**JILLY:** Oh, yes you can!
**JACK:** But I'm only a figment, remember?
**JILLY:** Figment or not, you are *not* sleeping with Sarah. You can sleep in the bath.
**JACK:** *(Aghast)* The bath!?
**JILLY:** *(Resolute)* The bath!
**JACK:** Couldn't I sleep in between you? It's a king size bed, so she'd never see me.
**JILLY:** No, but *you'd* see *her*.
**JACK:** So what? She wears a nightie, doesn't she?
**JILLY:** Er...no.
**JACK:** Pyjamas, eh?
**JILLY:** No.... she....
**JACK:** *(Suddenly interested)* She doesn't sleep *au naturel*?
**JILLY:** *(Angry)* No, she does not!
**JACK:** What, then?

**JILLY:** Never mind!
**JACK:** It can't be that bad. Tell me!
**JILLY:** You're a pervert!
**JACK:** True. But you might as well tell me. If you don't I might walk through the wall and have a peek for myself. She'd never know.
**JILLY:** You tried walking through the wall, remember? Not too successfully.
**JACK:** *(Impatient)* The door, then.
*(JILLY is lost for words.)*
**JACK:** Tell me!
**JILLY:** Why..? Why d'you want to know? It's no big secret!
**JACK:** In that case you won't mind telling me. It's only because you've made such a song and dance about it that I'm interested anyway.
**JILLY:** Liar!
**JACK:** Well...?
**JILLY:** Well..., if you must know.... she wears French knickers and a camisole.
**JACK:** Oh, is that all. Don't see what you made all the fuss about. You see more than that on the beach.
**JILLY:** A see-through camisole.
**JACK:** *(Eyes wide as his imagination runs riot; to himself)* Wow! *(After a pause; nonchalant; to Jilly)* Er.... what colour?
**JILLY:** What does it matter?
**JACK:** Just curious.
**JILLY:** Black, if you must know.
**JACK:** *(Gleeful)* I knew it! My favourite!
**JILLY:** Pervert!
**JACK:** Aren't I just!?
**JILLY:** I warn you, Jack, if you come anywhere near that bedroom I'll... I'll...
**JACK:** Kill me?
**JILLY:** Yes...! No...! Oh, I don't know, but I'll do something.
**JACK:** Not even a little peek?
**JILLY:** No! If you do I'll... I'll...
**JACK:** You'll what?
**JILLY:** I'll send Sarah home and invite my mother back!
**JACK:** *(Melodramatic)* No! No! Anything but that!
**JILLY:** *(Sensing victory)* In her long flannelette nighties!

**JACK:** O.K! O.K! I give in....! Can't I sleep on the settee, then? It's more comfortable than the bath.

**JILLY:** No. The bath it is.

**JACK:** Why?

**JILLY:** Because Sarah thinks I'm half crazy *now*. If she comes in and sees I've made a bed up in here she'll get them to cart me away to the asylum. So you sleep in the bath, where it's warm and you won't need covers. O.K?

**JACK:** *(Resigned)* I suppose so.

**JILLY:** No peeking?

**JACK:** No... no peeking!

**JILLY:** Not even a little one?

**JACK:** Not even a casual sideways glance through the door jamb if I just happened to be passing the bedroom door on the way to my ever-so-comfortable bathroom at the precise moment Sarah's getting ready for bed!

**JILLY:** I wish I could trust you.

**JACK:** You can. Have I ever lied to you?

**JILLY:** Frequently.

**JACK:** Ah, but that was when I was alive. Spirits can't lie, you know.

**JILLY:** Who says?

**JACK:** *I* say!

**JILLY:** That's a great comfort. How do I know you're not lying?

**JACK:** I told you... spirits can't.... Oh, I see what you mean. *(After a thought)* I'll prove it to you. Ask me a question. Any question. It doesn't matter how embarrassing.

**JILLY:** Don't be stupid!

**JACK:** Go on! Ask me something! Anything!

**JILLY:** Like what?

**JACK:** I don't know! Anyway, it's no use *me* choosing the questions. I could be cheating.

**JILLY:** Oh, I see... you can't *lie*, but you *can* cheat!

**JACK:** You know what I mean! Go on.... ask.

**JILLY:** Well.... I.... D'you.. er... do you like my mother?

**JACK:** *(Immediately)* No!

**JILLY:** Well, at least *that* had a ring of truth to it. No tact, but plenty of truth. What about your secretary?

**JACK:** What about her?

**JILLY:** Have you ever...? You know...

**JACK:** No, I *don't* know. What are you trying to imply...? That me and

## Wait Until The Ghost Is Clear

Dottie...? That Dottie and me...? *Jilly*, how could you!?

**JILLY:** So you didn't?

**JACK:** Emphatically *no*!

**JILLY:** Even if I've got proof otherwise?

**JACK:** You can't have! There *is* no proof. We've never done anything. I couldn't fancy Dottie if she were the last woman on Earth! Not that she's unattractive or anything. It's her voice. It makes her the least-fanciable woman I know.

**JILLY:** *(Victorious)* Ah! Got you!

**JACK:** What d'you mean?

**JILLY:** You told a lie!

**JACK:** I didn't! I tell you I don't fancy Dottie. For God's sake, she never shuts up!

**JILLY:** That's not the lie I meant!

**JACK:** No?

**JILLY:** No!

**JACK:** Then what...? I don't understand.

**JILLY:** You said Dottie is the least-fanciable woman you know.

**JACK:** So? I meant it.

**JILLY:** So... you'd prefer my mother, eh?

**JACK:** *(Aghast)* What!?

**JILLY:** If Dottie is the least-fanciable woman you know, that means my mother isn't.

**JACK:** I didn't mean that, I....

**JILLY:** You lied!

**JACK:** I didn't. It was just an expression.

**JILLY:** Liar!

**JACK:** Anyway, I'm not sure in all honesty that I class your mother as a woman.

**JILLY:** I knew I couldn't trust you!

**JACK:** You can, Jilly! Honestly.

**JILLY:** So tonight you're going to be locked in the bathroom.

**JACK:** *(Thinking fast)* But...but what if I need the toilet?

**JILLY:** Do spirits need toilets?

**JACK:** *(Thoughtful)* That's a point. I don't know. Not so far.

**JILLY:** So that's not a problem, is it?

**JACK:** But I don't want to sleep in there. It might be haunted.

**JILLY:** Yes.... by *you*!

51

## Wait Until The Ghost Is Clear

JACK: What if there's a fire? How would I get out?

JILLY: I always said you should burn in hell!

JACK: Jilly! Be serious!

JILLY: No, *you* be serious. Even if there *was* a fire, you can hardly burn to death, can you?

JACK: No, true, but....

JILLY: No buts. Any other desperate, but futile, attempts?

JACK: Well, I....

JILLY: Yes...?

JACK: *(Defeated)* No.

JILLY: Good. So at bedtime you can wait out here until Sarah and I have finished in the bathroom and then I'll lock you in.

JACK: *(A last glimmer of hope)* How will I know when you've finished? What if I accidentally came through too soon and I...?

JILLY: I'll come and get you when Sarah's safely tucked up in bed.

JACK: Spoilsport!

JILLY: *(Imitating Jack's earlier comment)* Aren't I just!?

JACK: But I won't be able to sleep in that bath. It's small and it's hard and the taps drip.

JILLY: Tough! You should have bought a two-bedroomed flat like I've often said.

JACK: What'll I do if I can't sleep?

JILLY: I have no idea. Read a book. Count sheep.

JACK: I'll see if I can get my walking-through-walls perfected!

JILLY: Just you dare!

JACK: A joke! Honestly!

*(They exit L as the CURTAIN falls.)*

## ACT III Scene 1

*(It is the following morning. As the curtain rises JILLY is speaking on the telephone. Her manner betrays that she has been talking for some time and is angry. She is dressed in "every day" clothes. During her telephone conversation SARAH enters L wearing a dressing gown and carrying a towel.)*

**JILLY:** *(Into the phone)* ...Yes, I know, Inspector.... I realise that, but.... *(With a sigh; defeated)* Oh, very well... Yes, I'll send them to you.... No... *(After another impatient sigh)* Alright, if you want to, but I can't promise there'll be anyone in... Yes. Goodbye. *(She slams the receiver down angrily and moves down R.)* Damn that woman!

**SARAH:** Inspector James?

**JILLY:** Who else?

**SARAH:** What's she want this time?

**JILLY:** *(Sitting in her armchair)* Jack's company books. They've been checking at his office and there's some missing. Probably the work Jack brought home before he... *(She trails off, unable to say "died".)*

**SARAH:** D'you know where they are?

**JILLY:** In the dining room, I expect. I'll find them later. They're sending someone over to pick them up.

**SARAH:** What does she want them for?

**JILLY:** I don't know. I've given up trying to second guess her.

**SARAH:** Probably just tying up loose ends. *(A pause; cautiously)* How's the er... figment?

**JILLY:** *(Terse)* I don't want to talk about him... it.

**SARAH:** *(Looking around the room)* Is he here?

**JILLY:** No.

**SARAH:** *(Brighter)* Then he's probably gone. I told you he would. A good night's sleep, that's all you needed.

**JILLY:** *(Weary)* Maybe you're right.

**SARAH:** Okay if I have a shower?

**JILLY:** *(Without thinking)* Yes, of course.

**SARAH:** *(Starting to the door L)* Thanks. Won't be long.

**JILLY:** *(Remembering)* No!

**SARAH:** *(Turning)* What?

**JILLY:** *(Rising; thinking fast)* You can't. It's er... it's broken.

**SARAH:** Broken..? But it was all right last night.

**JILLY:** *(On edge)* Well, it's not now.

**SARAH:** *(Moving towards her; suspicious)* Jilly... You can't fool me. I can tell when you're lying. What's going on?

**JILLY:** Nothing. Nothing.

**SARAH:** Has this got anything to do with your figment?

**JILLY:** *(Sitting; defeated)* Yes.

**SARAH:** Where is he?

**JILLY:** In the bathroom.

**SARAH:** *(Humouring her)* Have you seen him?

**JILLY:** No. I daren't go in.

**SARAH:** *(Losing patience; moving L)* Oh, once and for all, Jilly, this is ridiculous. You have your hallucinations if you want, but *I* need a shower. *(She exits L, leaving the door ajar.)*

**JILLY:** *(Rising and starting L)* Sarah! No...!

*(JILLY is about to exit L when the telephone rings. She looks at it, then the door, then rushes to answer the phone. She faces R.)*

**JILLY:** *(Sharply)* What...!? *(Calmer)* Oh, sorry, Mum... No, I... It was Sarah.... No, she.... *(Weary)* Nothing. It doesn't matter.... Yes, if you want... No, I'm all right, honestly...

*(In the middle of Jilly's telephone conversation JACK enters L and stands just inside the door. He is soaking wet and has a delighted but glazed look on his face. JILLY does not notice him and carries on with her conversation.)*

**JILLY:** No, really. I'm all right... Yes, come for coffee.... As soon as you like... Yes, okay. I'll see you later. 'Bye.

*(JILLY puts down the telephone slowly and is clearly troubled. Eventually she notices Jack standing there.)*

**JILLY:** Jack! What...!? *(She realises what he must have "seen" and advances on him, hand raised to strike)* You... you bastard!

**JACK:** *(Backing away, hands raised in self-protection)* Now, Jilly... You can't blame me.

*(Over the next few lines JILLY advances angrily towards JACK, who evades her by retreating behind the furniture.)*

**JILLY:** *(Fuming)* Oh, can't I?

**JACK:** No, you can't! It was *your* idea that I slept in the bath, not mine.

**JILLY:** *(Fuming)* Oooh!

**JACK:** It's not my fault.

**JILLY:** I suppose you.... she...?

**JACK:** *(Smiling at the memory)* Oh, yes. She did.

**JILLY:** You could have shut your eyes!

**JACK:** I couldn't...! I didn't have time! I was asleep, and all of a sudden she...

**JILLY:** I warn you, Jack... Whatever pathetic excuse you're about to dream up, I won't believe it.

**JACK:** It's true, Jilly. I was shattered. It took me ages to get to sleep last night. That bath isn't exactly comfortable, you know. I lay awake for hours. In the end I gave up and started trying to pick things up. *(Enthusiastic)* I actually managed to move the top of the toothpaste tube. Watch....!

*(JACK goes to the table and manages - with considerable concentration - to pick up a peanut, which he eats.)*

**JACK:** *(Pleased with himself)* There! How about that?

**JILLY:** *(Unimpressed)* Simply wonderful. Now stop trying to change the subject!

**JACK:** I wasn't... I must have eventually dropped off.... I don't remember anything until a few minutes ago when Sarah burst in, flung off her dressing gown, trampled all over me and turned on the shower. *(After mentally recalling the vision)* What an odd place to have a birthmark.

**JILLY:** Tart!

**JACK:** Now that's not fair! She wasn't to know I was there, was she? *(Hopeful)* Unless, of course you *have* made all this up?

**JILLY:** I *told* her you were there!

**JACK:** And did she believe you?

**JILLY:** No. She said I was having hallucinations.

**JACK:** Perhaps you are. Perhaps I'm not really here at all.

**JILLY:** Now don't start all that again. I was laying in bed last night and I thought to myself... "Jilly," I thought... "Pull yourself together. Like Sarah said, it *was* a hard day." So I convinced myself she was right - you were an hallucination. I went to sleep thinking that I'd wake up and you'd be gone. *(Sitting in the armchair; with an angry sob)* But you're not! You're still here!

**JACK:** *(Sitting on the settee)* It's nice to be wanted.

**JILLY:** Why *are* you here, Jack!? Why!?

**JACK:** *I* don't know! *(After a moment's silence; unsure of himself)* Jilly...

**JILLY:** What!?

**JACK:** I can't be absolutely certain... But last night, just as I was dozing off, I had a most peculiar experience. You know people say they've had an "out-of-body experience"..? Well, it was just like that. It was sort of like being here, but being... somewhere else as well... Almost as if I was looking down on myself... *(He trails off.)*

**JILLY:** *(Impatient)* Well?

**JACK:** Well, there was someone there with me - *(as if remembering a*

# Wait Until The Ghost Is Clear

*dream)* I can't remember who it was, it was all too vague - but whoever it was told me I'd been sent back to bring my killer to justice.

**JILLY:** Your killer...? Then you *are* a ghost!

**JACK:** Looks like it.

**JILLY:** You don't sound very upset about it.

**JACK:** What's the point? I'm dead and gone.... Except I'm not. I'm back.

**JILLY:** *(Hesitant)* And... Just how are you supposed to do it..? "Bring your killer to justice"?

**JACK:** I don't know... Nobody told me.

**JILLY:** *(Even more hesitant)* And er... who exactly *was* your killer?

**JACK:** That's just it. I don't know.

**JILLY:** *(Less tense)* You don't know?

**JACK:** No. It was dark. I didn't see.

**JILLY:** What exactly *do* you remember?

**JACK:** Not much. I was here, cleaning my gun and talking to you, then it all went dark.

**JILLY:** The lights went out.

**JACK:** In more ways than one. The next thing I remember is being back here on the settee, almost as if nothing had happened. It was almost as if I'd blacked out for a split second. Just as if I'd blinked.

**JILLY:** Don't you remember *anything* about the last two weeks?

**JACK:** No. Not a thing. It was just as if I'd not moved. That's why I was so surprised when Sarah suddenly appeared.

**JILLY:** How come it's only me that can see you?

**JACK:** Perhaps you're my murderer.

**JILLY:** *(Offended)* Jack! How can you!?

**JACK:** You were the one checking my life insurance policies.

**JILLY:** Well I didn't! *(After a long pause)* Would you be mad at me if I was?

**JACK:** What? My killer?

**JILLY:** Mmmm.

**JACK:** That's a damn silly question, isn't it? It's not exactly the sort of thing that's easy to be calm about. Are you trying to tell me that you...?

**JILLY:** No, course not. I was just curious, that's all.

**JACK:** Anyway, we don't know that you *are* the only one who can see me. We only know that you *can* and Sarah *can't*.

**JILLY:** Yes... I see what you mean.

**JACK:** Maybe Sarah's the killer.

**JILLY:** *(Incredulous)* What!? Sarah!? Why should she want to kill you?

**JACK:** I don't know. Jealousy perhaps.

**JILLY:** Jealousy!?

**JACK:** Yes. Perhaps she thought that if she couldn't have me, nobody would.

**JILLY:** *(Standing; incredulous)* I don't believe it! Death hasn't exactly blunted your ego, has it?

**JACK:** It's possible.

**JILLY:** *(Firm)* No.... it isn't!

**JACK:** Alright... I'm just exploring all possibilities.

**JILLY:** That's what that Police Inspector said.

**JACK:** What Police Inspector?

**JILLY:** Inspector James.

**JACK:** Inspector James? Never heard of him. James who?

**JILLY:** Hah! Typical man! When anyone says "Police Inspector" you automatically assume it's a man.

**JACK:** *(Aghast)* You mean it's not?

**JILLY:** No, she's not.

**JACK:** You mean she's a woman?

**JILLY:** Very astute deduction, councillor! James is her surname.

**JACK:** *(Rising and moving L)* God help us! No wonder they've sent *me* back to solve the case.

**JILLY:** Chauvinist!

**JACK:** *(Turning)* No... realist!

**JILLY:** Death hasn't changed you much at all, has it? You're still the same egotistical, pig-headed, ignorant....

**JACK:** *(Interrupting; shaking his head)* You can't be serious!

**JILLY:** *(Returning to her original question)* Why *should* she have killed you?

**JACK:** *(Moving C)* The Policewoman?

**JILLY:** No, stupid! Sarah! *(A thought occurs to her. With menace creeping into her voice)* Jack..! You and Sarah... Sarah and you...? You weren't...? Were you?

**JACK:** *(Puzzled)* Jilly, you never made much sense when you were alive, but...

**JILLY:** I *am* alive... It's *you* that's dead!

**JACK:** *(Impatient)* Whatever.... But, what I mean is.... What the hell are you talking about?

## Wait Until The Ghost Is Clear

**JILLY:** I'm asking you if you and Sarah were, sort of, *seeing* each other.

**JACK:** *(Shocked)* Sarah and me...!? Me and Sarah...!? *(His expression changes)* What a wonderful idea!

**JILLY:** *(Furious)* Jack!

*(JILLY slaps Jack on the shoulder, knocking him sideways onto the settee.)*

**JACK:** Ow..! Jilly!

**JILLY:** *(Sneering)* Didn't feel a thing.

**JACK:** *(Rubbing his shoulder)* Well *I* did.

**JILLY:** You'd better be careful what you say to me, then. I can hit you as hard as I like, remember, and it's only *you* that feels it!

**JACK:** That's not fair.

**JILLY:** You're the lawyer... Sue me! *(Raising her hand to strike again)* Now, answer my question!

**JACK:** What question?

**JILLY:** *(Ready to strike; warning)* Jack..

**JACK:** *(Shielding himself)* Alright! Alright...! No... we didn't.

**JILLY:** Honestly? You never had any improper goings on behind my back?

**JACK:** That's a quaint way of putting it.

**JILLY:** Jack... I warn you!

**JACK:** No, we didn't. I've never laid a finger on her.

**JILLY:** Or she on you?

**JACK:** No...! Apart from this morning, that is.

**JILLY:** What d'you mean?

**JACK:** When she was getting in the shower she nearly knocked my eyes out.

**JILLY:** Don't be disgusting!

**JACK:** She did! She swung her elbow round and clouted me.

**JILLY:** Oh... I see. I thought you meant with her.... her... chest!

**JACK:** I should be so lucky. Trouble is, when people can't see or feel you they don't hold back!

**JILLY:** No... So she had no reason to kill you? *(She sits.)*

**JACK:** None that I can think of. *(After a pause)* I still think it was you.

**JILLY:** It was *not* me! Why should I?

**JACK:** Well, you hated me, for one.

**JILLY:** Yes, but apart from that, why should I?

**JACK:** *(Rising; accusing)* Because you've got a boyfriend!

**JILLY:** *(Aghast)* I what!?

**JACK:** You heard.

**JILLY:** I heard... I just didn't believe!

**JACK:** Go on, admit it. You both wanted me out of the way.

**JILLY:** Jack, if I had a boyfriend....

**JACK:** Aha!

**JILLY:** ...*If* I had a boyfriend, and *if* we wanted you out of the way.... A perfectly understandable thing to want in view of the irrational way you behave... I could just have left you. Or thrown you out.

**JACK:** And get cut off without a penny? Hah!

**JILLY:** As far as *I* was aware when you were alive that would have been all I got. A couple of thousand quidsworth of life insurance and the mortgage on this flat. Big deal!

**JACK:** There's the business.

**JILLY:** The business!? I wouldn't have got anything out of that. Apart from the fact that it never seems to make any money....

**JACK:** That's not true!

**JILLY:** Apart from that, Walter gets control, if you remember. You both agreed that when you set it up.

**JACK:** *(Pensive)* Walter... *(He sits.)*

**JILLY:** And I didn't know anything about that last insurance policy, so you can hardly say that was a motive.

**JACK:** What last insurance policy?

**JILLY:** The one you took out two days before you died.

**JACK:** What..? You're mad. I've not taken out any insurance for years.

**JILLY:** The policy was in your safe deposit box.

**JACK:** Rubbish!

**JILLY:** It was! Three hundred thousand pounds in the event of your death.

**JACK:** *(Flabbergasted) How much!?*

**JILLY:** A third of a million pounds.

**JACK:** But... but that's crazy. It must be a mistake.

**JILLY:** Inspector James doesn't seem to think so.

**JACK:** It must be a forgery. You've got to tell her.

**JILLY:** Oh, yes. I'm sure she'll believe me. "Inspector, my dead husband has come back to haunt me and he's told me his insurance policy's a forgery"! They'll cart me away in a van!

**JACK:** But don't you see..? It's a vital clue! Whoever took out that policy has to be the killer!

**JILLY:** I know. That's what I tried to tell her! But we don't know who

## Wait Until The Ghost Is Clear

took it out.

**JACK:** But it's obvious. Whoever benefits from the policy is the killer.

**JILLY:** *(Stopped in her tracks)* Ah!

**JACK:** What!? Who is it? Tell me!

**JILLY:** Me!

**JACK:** You!?

**JILLY:** Me.

**JACK:** *(After a pause)* I thought it was you all along!

**JILLY:** Jack! Will you be serious for once in your life!?

**JACK:** *(Rising)* A bit late for that, don't you think!?

**JILLY:** It wasn't *me*! As if I'd be stupid enough to take out a huge policy on you, leave it for all to find in your safe deposit box, and then kill you. I didn't even know you *had* a safe deposit box.

**JACK:** Did you tell the Police that?

**JILLY:** Of course I told them. But they don't believe me. They're firmly convinced *I* did it.

**JACK:** *(Pensive again) Nobody* knew about that box. Nobody.

**JILLY:** Somebody must have done.

**JACK:** Yes. But who?

**JILLY:** *(Sitting on the armchair; a hint of desperation)* What're we going to do, Jack?

**JACK:** I don't know, Jilly. I really don't.

**JILLY:** You won't let them take me away, will you?

**JACK:** *(Sitting on the arm of the chair and putting his arm around her)* No, Jilly. I won't let them take you away.

*(JILLY lets her head rest on the chair against Jack's chest. He strokes her hair. They are a couple in love again. They are silent for a few moments.)*

**JILLY:** Jack...

**JACK:** What is it?

**JILLY:** What's it like in the spirit world?

**JACK:** Ask your Mum. The amount of gin she puts away she's bound to know!

**JILLY:** Ohhh! *(She gives him a lovers' tap.)* I mean it.

**JACK:** I don't remember. I just feel as if I've never been away. Except that nobody can see or hear me.

**JILLY:** Except for me.

**JACK:** Except for you. And nobody believes you.

**JILLY:** Except for you.

## Wait Until The Ghost Is Clear

**JACK:** A great couple we make, don't we? Perhaps we've *both* gone mad.
*(The doorbell rings. JILLY starts.)*
**JILLY:** Who's that?
**JACK:** *I* don't know. Shall I go?
**JILLY:** It's probably Mum.
**JACK:** *(Rising)* Then I *will* go. *(Moving L)* This way.
**JILLY:** No you won't! Sarah's out there..., so you stay here... where I can keep an eye on you!
**JACK:** *(In a complaining whine)* Jilly...!
**JILLY:** *(Pointing to the settee; like a dog-owner)* Sit!
*(JACK sits obediently.)*
**JACK:** *(Imitating a begging dog)* Do I get a dog-biscuit now?
**JILLY:** Later.... if you're a good boy.
*(JILLY exits R and the door is heard to open off R.)*
**EDNA:** *(Off R)* Hello, darling... How are you?
*(The door closes off R. JILLY enters, followed by EDNA.)*
**JILLY:** *(As she enters)* Oh, I'm much better now. *(With a pointed look at Jack)* Things are *much* clearer.
**EDNA:** What was all that about Sarah?
**JILLY:** *(Puzzled)* Sarah?
**EDNA:** Yes. You sounded really upset on the phone. You said something about Sarah.
**JILLY:** Did I?
**EDNA:** Yes.
**JILLY:** Well, whatever it was I can't remember. Why don't you sit down? Would you like a drink?
**JACK:** Stupid question! *(To Edna)* Tea...? Coffee...? Sulphuric Acid?
**EDNA:** A small gin would be nice. With a splash of tonic.
**JACK:** At nine-thirty in the morning!?
**JILLY:** Let me take your coat.
**JACK:** No, don't... She might decide to stay.
*(JILLY casts a withering look at Jack and takes Edna's coat. EDNA goes to the settee and is about to sit on Jack, who stands quickly. JILLY takes the coat off R. JACK wanders up L.)*
**EDNA:** *(Calling to off R)* Have you been out?
**JILLY:** *(Entering R)* No... Why?
*(JILLY pours a gin and tonic and hands it to Edna.)*
**EDNA:** Your phone was engaged. I've been trying to get through to you

## Wait Until The Ghost Is Clear

for ages.
**JACK:** It's a lost cause, Edna. *I've* been trying to get through to her for years.
**EDNA:** Are you alright?
**JILLY:** Yes.
**EDNA:** Four times, I rang. I began to worry something might be wrong, so I came round...
**JACK:** And now something is!
**JILLY:** *(Sitting in the armchair)* No, I'm okay. Honestly.
*(JACK spots the spider on the floor L. He starts towards it.)*
**JACK:** *(To Jilly)* Jilly! It's that blasted spider!
*(JACK starts spider hunting.)*
**JILLY:** *(Frowning at Jack; to Edna, suddenly angry at the memory)* It was probably that *bloody* Police Inspector. She's called three times already today.
**EDNA:** Now, now, Gillian! I know you're upset, but there's no need for vulgarity.
**JACK:** *(Excited)* Jilly, it's not moving. Obviously it can't see me. I just hope it's as light as the peanuts! *(He is on his hands and knees.)*
**JILLY:** She thinks I killed Jack.
**EDNA:** Of course she doesn't.
**JILLY:** She as good as said so.
**EDNA:** Now, Gillian, you're just being hysterical.
**JILLY:** Everything points to me. Everything!
*(JACK makes a grab for the spider.)*
**EDNA:** Nonsense.
**JACK:** *(Standing; his hand clenched)* Got it!
**JILLY:** *(Thoughtful)* Only one thing.... Jack left *you* some money in his will!
**EDNA:** *(Surprised)* He what!?
**JILLY:** He left you two thousand pounds.
**EDNA:** *(Amazed)* Jack..? He left *me* some money!? Why?
**JILLY:** I wish I knew. *(Without thinking; pointedly at Jack)* I must ask him.
**EDNA:** *Ask* him!?
**JILLY:** *(Realising what she has said)* Er... Walter. I must ask Walter. He helped Jack to do his will. He's bound to know.
**EDNA:** I can't believe it. I thought he despised me.
**JACK:** Very perceptive!

## Wait Until The Ghost Is Clear

**JILLY:** *(Trying to get Jack to tell her)* I'd *love* to know what was in his mind when he wrote that.

**JACK:** Simple, my love. I'm a kind, generous person.

**JILLY:** Perhaps he was just being kind and generous.

**EDNA:** Jack!? Never! He was about as kind and generous as a Tax Inspector with an ulcer.

**JACK:** Charming!

**JILLY:** Mother! Don't talk about Jack like that. He might hear you.

**EDNA:** Where he's gone he'll be too busy attending to his third degree burns!

**JILLY:** You don't know that. He could be anywhere.

**EDNA:** Nonsense!

**JILLY:** He could be here... in this room... right now.

**EDNA:** Don't be ridiculous, Gillian.

**JACK:** Yes, don't be silly, Jilly.

**JILLY:** You never know.

**EDNA:** Are you trying to tell me that you've started believing in ghosts?

**JILLY:** I keep an open mind about it.

**EDNA:** You're insane! *(After a pause; curious)* Two thousand pounds, eh..? *(Pensive)* But why..? What was he up to?

**JACK:** *(Moving C)* I left her a bit because I didn't want the conniving old boot pestering you for money every ten minutes after I died.

**JILLY:** I'm sure he left you the money because he didn't want to think of you accepting charity from me after he died.

**JACK:** That wasn't what I said.

**EDNA:** After all, I hardly need his money!

**JILLY:** You ought to be grateful! Whatever you thought of him while he was alive, you shouldn't think ill of the dead.

**JACK:** *(To Jilly; glancing at Edna)* Does that have to work both ways?

**EDNA:** Yes, darling, you're right of course.

*(EDNA raises her glass in a toast. Unseen by the women, before Edna can drink, JACK drops the spider in it.)*

**EDNA:** *(Not noticing; looking heavenwards)* To Jack... wherever you are...

**JACK:** *(Next to her)* Right here, Edna!

**EDNA:** *(Grandly)* ...I salute you.... More generous in death than ever in life.

**JILLY:** Mum! That's awful!

**EDNA:** I'm quite sure if the situation were reversed Jack would be exactly the same about me.

**JACK:** *(R of Edna)* If there was any gin left.

**EDNA:** Aren't you having one?

**JILLY:** Not this early, thanks. I was just going to make a coffee for Sarah and me.

**EDNA:** Suit yourself. Cheers. *(She is about to drink when she notices the spider.)* Aaargh! *(She starts, throwing the drink all over Jack.)* There's a spider in my drink!

**JACK:** *(Annoyed)* Oh, for God's sake!

**JILLY:** *(To Jack)* Serves you right!

**EDNA:** What!?

**JILLY:** *(Rising and moving to Edna)* Er... I said... "Are you all right?"

**EDNA:** It was horrible! You know how I hate spiders.

**JILLY:** Never mind. It's gone now. *(Taking the glass)* D'you want another?

**EDNA:** No. I couldn't. *(She shudders.)* I don't think I shall ever touch gin again.

**JACK:** Now that *is* difficult to believe. And she thinks *you're* mad for believing in ghosts!

**EDNA:** I'll have that coffee with you and Sarah. Where is she, by the way?

**JILLY:** In the shower. *(Moving to the door L. She opens it and calls)* Sarah!

**SARAH:** *(Off L; distant)* Yes!?

**JILLY:** I'm making a coffee. D'you want one?

**SARAH:** Please. I'll be out in a few minutes.

**EDNA:** *(Rising)* I'll come and help you.

**JACK:** I'll go and check Sarah's okay.

*(EDNA exits L. JILLY follows. JACK goes to follow, but JILLY - with a smug smile - closes the door in his face before he can exit. He takes hold of the handle and tries to open it, but no matter how hard he tries he cannot. Just as he is about to give up SARAH opens the door suddenly and knocks him flying. JACK is so busy picking himself up that he does not notice at first that SARAH is dressed in very sexy black lingerie. She carries a packet of stockings and a make-up bag.)*

**JACK:** Why don't you watch where you're going you stupid....? *(Now he notices.)* Wow!

*(SARAH enters the room, puts the stockings and the bag on the sideboard, opens the bag and checks her already immaculate make-up in the mirror L. JACK moves to her. He puts out a hand towards various desirable parts of her body and wonders if he dare touch. Several times he decides against it, but*

## Wait Until The Ghost Is Clear

*instead strokes her hair. SARAH carries on totally unaware.)*
**JACK:** This being a ghost has it's perks!
**JILLY:** *(Calling from off L)* Sarah!
*(JACK jumps like a scared rabbit and, looking warily at the door L moves rapidly away from Sarah. He sits in his usual place on the settee.)*
**SARAH:** *(Calling)* Yes?
**JILLY:** *(Off L)* D'you want any breakfast?
**SARAH:** No thanks. Just coffee.
*(SARAH unwraps the stockings and moves to the settee. She puts one foot on the settee between Jack's legs and proceeds to roll on her stocking and fasten her suspenders. JACK is agog. When she has put the first on she repeats the process with the other leg.)*
**JACK:** *(Relaxing back, hands behind his head)* So this is what Heaven is like!
*(SARAH stands and returns to the mirror L. JACK watches her, then eventually rises and stands next to her again. He is transfixed and starts to lower her shoulder strap when, unseen by him, JILLY enters L carrying Sarah's cup of coffee. As JILLY sees what Jack is about to do she storms over to him and slaps him roundly across the back. Jack is knocked sideways.)*
**JACK:** Ow!
*(SARAH senses Jilly's movement and turns questioningly.)*
**SARAH:** Jilly! What are you doing?
**JILLY:** Er... It was a mosquito. It's gone now.
**JACK:** *(To Jilly)* Mosquito!?
**JILLY:** *(Sotto voce in reply)* Perhaps I should have said "Rat"!
**SARAH:** *(Half hearing)* What?
*(JILLY gives Sarah her coffee.)*
**JILLY:** *(Disapproving)* I said "D'you have to wander around the flat dressed like *that*?"
**SARAH:** *(Puzzled by her hostility)* Yes, whyever not?
**JILLY:** You look as if you're out to satisfy every man's fantasies.
**SARAH:** What?
**JILLY:** Your.... *(She does not complete the sentence but waves vaguely at Sarah's lingerie.)*
**SARAH:** Nonsense! I don't wear things like this for men. *I* like them. They make me feel feminine.
**JACK:** *(Sitting on the downstage end of the settee)* And how!
*(JILLY glares at him.)*

**JILLY:** Jack was always threatening to buy me things like that. He did once.

**JACK:** *(To Sarah)* And Jilly always threatened to throw them straight in the bin!

**SARAH:** That's nice.

**JILLY:** *(Sitting in the armchair; surprised at her attitude)* Nice!? I went mad!

**SARAH:** *(Moving next to Jilly)* Why?

**JILLY:** I couldn't go around dressed like that!

**JACK:** Couldn't...? *Wouldn't*, you mean.

**SARAH:** *(Sitting on the upstage end of the settee)* Why not? What harm could it have done?

**JILLY:** *(Defensive)* That's not the point. That's all men ever think about... Dressing their women up just to suit their own perverse desires! Selfish!

**JACK:** Selfish!? Me!?

**SARAH:** I think that's very sad.

**JILLY:** Sad? Why sad?

**SARAH:** Like I said, what harm could it have done? Jack would've liked it, and if you're honest it wouldn't really have hurt you, would it?

**JILLY:** No, but...

**SARAH:** You may even got something out of it yourself, like I do... There's no harm in that. These stockings may be expensive, but they feel gorgeous. *(Stretching her leg forward)* Just feel.
*(JACK reaches towards Sarah's leg. JILLY quickly leans over and pulls his hand away, touching Sarah's leg for the briefest moment possible.)*

**JILLY:** *(Curt)* Yes... very nice. *(She sits back.)*

**SARAH:** Perhaps if you'd both been a bit more considerate with one another you wouldn't have argued so much... Wouldn't have felt so guilty.

**JILLY:** *(Incredulous)* Guilty!? Me!?

**SARAH:** You can't fool me, Jilly... I know you too well. You miss him.

**JILLY:** Of course I miss him!

**JACK:** *(Slightly surprised)* You do?

**SARAH:** And you feel guilty because you're thinking of all the things you should have been doing and saying to each other while you actually spent the time fighting.

**JACK:** *(Seeing the light)* She's right, you know, Jilly.

**SARAH:** And now it's too late. He's gone.

**JILLY:** Don't be too sure of that.

**SARAH:** Now don't start that again.
**JACK:** You'll have to tell her.
**JILLY:** *(She stands. After a pause; taking a deep breath)* He's still here, Sarah.
**SARAH:** *(Reaching the end of her patience)* Oh, for God's sake!
**JILLY:** That's why I didn't want you wandering around dressed like that.
**SARAH:** *(Controlling herself)* Jilly.... Sit down.

*(JILLY sits on the armchair. SARAH stands in front of her. JACK rises and stands up C.)*

**JILLY:** I know what you're going to say, Sarah, but whether I'm going mad or not he's still here.
**SARAH:** *(Not knowing how to address the situation; after a pause)* Where is he?
**JACK:** I'm here!
**JILLY:** There... Standing next to you.
**SARAH:** If he is there, and I'm only saying "*if*" for the moment, how come it's only you that can see him?
**JILLY:** *(Standing) I* don't know! It's never happened to me before.
**SARAH:** *(After a pause during which she doubts her own sanity)* Ask Jack if *he* knows.

*(JILLY looks questioningly at JACK.)*

**JACK:** *(With a shrug)* Search me.
**JILLY:** He says he doesn't know.
**SARAH:** Can you touch him?
**JILLY:** Oh, yes. I gave him a right clout before. You remember... the mosquito? *I* didn't feel a thing, but *Jack* did!
**SARAH:** So that's what you were doing.
**JILLY:** Yes. I won't tell you what *he* was doing!
**SARAH:** Can *he* touch *you*?
**JILLY:** No. he keeps trying, but he can't. Or at least, when he does I can't feel it. The best he's managed so far is picking up the top of the toothpaste tube.
**JACK:** *(Smug)* Don't forget the spider! And the nuts!
**SARAH:** Can he touch me?
**JILLY:** That's the bit I wasn't going to tell you about!
**SARAH:** Oh, I see.... I didn't *feel* anything.
**JILLY:** *(Glaring at Jack)* Just as well for him!
**JACK:** *(Defensive)* I never touched her. Honest!

# Wait Until The Ghost Is Clear

**SARAH:** Get him to try.
**JILLY:** What?
**SARAH:** Touching me.
**JILLY:** What!?
**JACK:** *(Rubbing his hands in glee)* Oh, yes!
**SARAH:** You do want me to believe you, don't you?
**JILLY:** Yes, but...
**SARAH:** Then get him to try. I can't hear him, I can't see him. Maybe we can make physical contact.
**JACK:** *(To Sarah)* Why d'you have to wait till I'm dead to make a suggestion like that?
**JILLY:** Behave!
**SARAH:** What did he say?
**JILLY:** You don't want to know. *(Realising she has no alternative; she sighs)* Very well. *(To Jack)* Go on.
**JACK:** *(With a smile)* Really?
**JILLY:** *(Threatening)* And keep it clean! No naughty bits! *(To Sarah)* Keep very still.
**SARAH:** *(Standing upright and looking uneasy)* I can't believe I'm doing this.

*(JACK starts towards Sarah's bust.)*

**JILLY:** *(Warning)* Jack!
**JILLY:** *(Taking his hand away)* Just joking!

*(JACK touches Sarah's arm. SARAH shows no reaction.)*

**JACK:** *(Glancing from Sarah to Jilly)* Anything?
**JILLY:** Anything?
**SARAH:** No. Not a thing. Where's he touching?
**JILLY:** Your boobs.
**SARAH:** *(Suddenly enraged)* What!?
**JILLY:** *(Helpful)* He's behind you.

*(SARAH whirls round and slaps Jack. The hit is imprecise, because she cannot "see" him, but JACK is knocked sideways.)*

**JACK:** Ow!
**JILLY:** *(Amused)* Great shot! He certainly felt *that*!
**JACK:** *(To Jilly)* What did you say that for? I only touched her arm.
**JILLY:** You deserved it.
**SARAH:** What?
**JILLY:** He deserved that. He was only touching your arm, really, but his

mind was elsewhere!

*(JACK sulkily picks up a peanut and eats it. Over the next few lines he cannot keep his eyes off Sarah.)*

**SARAH:** I didn't feel anything, Jilly. You've got to face the possibility that all this *may* be in your mind.

**JILLY:** *(Desperate)* It's not, Sarah. I *know* it's not. Why won't anyone believe me? *(She resumes her seat.)*

**SARAH:** Because it's so unbelievable, that's why.

**JILLY:** So you think I'm crazy?

**SARAH:** *(Sitting on the settee)* I don't know what to think. I really don't.

**JILLY:** D'you think I should contact a priest or something?

**SARAH:** Maybe... Or how about that woman next door but one to me? Mrs Ball. She claims to be a medium.

**JILLY:** That small fat woman?

**JACK:** She's no medium. Extra large at least.

**SARAH:** Yes, that's the one. Not that I believe in all that rubbish myself.

**JILLY:** *(After a gloomy pause)* Sarah... Even though you don't believe me, will you do something for me?

**SARAH:** What?

**JILLY:** Go and get properly dressed. Even if Jack's eyes *are* only in my imagination, at the moment they're out on stalks. If he wasn't already dead I'd be worried about him having a heart attack.

**JACK:** *(Eating another peanut)* Spoilsport!

**SARAH:** *(Rising)* All right. I'll go. *(She moves L.)*

*(JACK moves towards the door L. As he does so, SARAH's gaze follows him. She looks concerned.)*

**JILLY:** What...!? What is it!?

**SARAH:** I... It's nothing, but I....

**JILLY:** *(Standing; excited)* What!?

**SARAH:** I could have sworn I saw.... *(Dismissive)* No, it's ridiculous.

**JILLY:** *(Impatient)* Jack..!? You saw Jack!?

**SARAH:** No. A peanut... Being chewed... In mid air.

**JILLY:** That was him! He just ate one! Sarah... you saw him!

**SARAH:** *(Shaking her head to clear it)* I think I'm going as mad as you are! I'm going to change.

**JACK:** One last twirl before you go, Sarah.

**JILLY:** Sarah.

**SARAH:** *(Turning at the door L; still troubled)* Yes?

## Wait Until The Ghost Is Clear

**JILLY:** Don't say anything to Mum, will you? She won't be as understanding as you are.

**SARAH:** Mum's the word. *(She exits L.)*

**JACK:** *(Resuming his usual seat, where Sarah had been sitting)* Lovely. Still warm!

**JILLY:** *(To Jack; excited)* Jack..! She saw you!

**JACK:** *(Eating a peanut)* She saw my nuts.

*(The doorbell rings off R.)*

**JILLY:** *(Nervous)* Who's that?

**JACK:** How am *I* supposed to know? I haven't perfected seeing through walls.... Yet.

**JILLY:** Just as well. For Sarah's sake!

**JACK:** Go and see.

**JILLY:** It might be the killer.

**JACK:** Which means it could be anyone.

**JILLY:** *(Moving to him)* Jack, I'm scared.

**JACK:** *(Standing; calming)* Stop worrying. I told you... I'll look after you.

**JILLY:** Promise?

**JACK:** I promise. Now go and answer the door. I'd go myself, but whoever it is may not want to see me... Even if they could.

(JILLY exits R, leaving it ajar. JACK goes towards the door and listens. The door off R opens.)

**JILLY:** *(Off R)* Walter!

**WALTER:** *(Off R)* Hi, Jilly. How are you?

**JILLY:** All right, I suppose. I've been better. Come in.

*(JILLY and WALTER enter R.)*

**WALTER:** *(As he enters)* I won't keep you long, love. I know you're still upset.

**JILLY:** I'm all right. Really I am.

**WALTER:** You know, I was thinking... Don't think wrongly of me, but now Jack's... gone, perhaps you and I... one night when you're feeling better, of course, perhaps we could... have a meal together or something.

**JACK:** Judas! How dare you!? Tell him where to go, Jilly.

**JILLY:** Walter! It's a bit soon to be saying things like that. Jack's hardly even settled in his grave!

**WALTER:** I know, but... well... when you're feeling better, perhaps.

**JACK:** Over my dead body!

**JILLY:** We'll see, Walter. We'll see.

## Wait Until The Ghost Is Clear

**WALTER:** Yes, okay.
**JILLY:** Was there something you wanted?
**JACK:** Apart from trying to steal your best mate's widow, that is!?
**WALTER:** Oh, yes. *(Tentatively)* Have you by any chance found any papers from the office? Jack brought some home the day he....
**JILLY:** Some books?
**WALTER:** That's right. Have you got them?
**JILLY:** Oh, I've been meaning to look for those. The Police want them.
**JACK:** *(Pensive)* The books! Of course!
**WALTER:** *(Guarded)* The Police? What do they want them for?
**JILLY:** I don't know. They want everything. I don't know why they don't just send a removal van round and clear out the flat!
**WALTER:** *(Suddenly threatening)* Don't give them to them!
**JILLY:** *(Surprised at his sudden change of manner)* What!?
**WALTER:** *I* want them.
**JACK:** Jilly... Don't give them to him! I remember now. It was the books.
**JILLY:** The books?
**WALTER:** *(Impatient)* Yes, the books. Where are they?
**JACK:** Stall him. I'll get help. *(He rushes off L.)*
**JILLY:** I er... I haven't got them.
**JACK:** *(Off L; calling)* Sarah! Sarah! Help! It's Jilly. Edna! Somebody help!
*(WALTER pulls his gun from his jacket and points it at JILLY.)*
**JILLY:** Walter...! What...!?
**WALTER:** *(Grabbing her wrist)* Not a word! Scream out and I'll shoot you. Now where are those books?
**JILLY:** *(Pointing at the sideboard; terrified)* In there.
*(JACK enters L. WALTER releases Jilly's wrist and threatens her with the gun.)*
**WALTER:** Stay there!
*(JACK goes to Jilly and motions for her to keep calm and quiet. WALTER searches the sideboard and gets the books.)*
**JACK:** Keep him talking.
**JILLY:** *Why*, Walter? What are you doing?
**WALTER:** I need these books, Jilly. Why couldn't you just have given them to me?
*(JACK motions for Jilly to keep going, and frantically paces about wondering what he can do.)*

## Wait Until The Ghost Is Clear

**JILLY:** But why? What for?

**WALTER:** I'm in trouble. The partnership was hard up for cash and I made a few deals with some rather nasty people.

**JILLY:** What sort of deals?

**JACK:** *(He suddenly has an idea)* Jilly, stall him! Whatever you do, just keep talking! *(He rushes off L.)*

**WALTER:** They supplied the money and I... had a word with one or two court officials and some jurors.

**JILLY:** *(Aghast)* You....? And Jack, was he...?

**WALTER:** *(With a wry smile)* Jack? Huh! No, Jack was as pure as the driven snow. Jack worked hard and long and believed that everything would work out. Jack only ever wanted two things.... a quiet little partnership.. and *you*.

**JILLY:** Me?

**WALTER:** Yes. *(Shaking his head in regret)* Why did he have to go delving into those books?

**JILLY:** *(Realising; with a look of horror)* You... you killed him.

**WALTER:** I had no choice. He would've found out. I'd have been ruined. *(He moves to the door L and closes it, standing next to it.)*

**JILLY:** Oh, Walter! Walter! He'd have done anything for you. Why didn't you tell him?

**WALTER:** I couldn't, Jilly. I was in too deep. I'm sorry, Jilly.... *(He raises his gun.)*

**JILLY:** *(Stalling)* Walter... I've got to know... How did you do it? With his own gun? He'd been cleaning it... It wasn't loaded.

**WALTER:** It was *my* gun he was cleaning... I'd switched them earlier.

**JILLY:** Then you planned it!

**WALTER:** I knew he was suspicious. Don't you see...? I had no choice. After I'd shot him I switched them back again.

**JILLY:** My God! *(A pause.)* And now...?

**WALTER:** I'm sorry, Jilly. You know too much.

**JILLY:** *(Backing away and holding her hands up as if to shield her)* Walter, no! Mum's outside... and Sarah... Sarah's upstairs... You can't..! *(In a wail)* Jack...!

*(The timing of the next entries must be fast and precise. WALTER slowly raises the pistol and aims at Jilly. As Jilly screams SARAH enters L and the door knocks WALTER sideways as he shoots. An ornament shatters, hit by the stray bullet. As he is about to recover EDNA enters L past Sarah carrying a frying pan. JACK follows. EDNA sees Walter getting up and knocks him on the head with her pan. WALTER collapses unconscious on the floor.)*

## Wait Until The Ghost Is Clear

**JILLY:** *(Breathing hard)* Oh, my God!

**SARAH:** *(Going to Jilly)* Jilly, what happened?

**JILLY:** Walter! He's the killer. He was going to kill me.

**EDNA:** What!?

**JILLY:** Thank God you came in when you did.

**SARAH:** *(Puzzled)* Yes, it was peculiar, that. I was just finishing getting dressed when I was hit on the head with the top of a toothpaste tube. Then I happened to notice them... on the floor.

**JILLY:** What?

**SARAH:** *(Troubled; looking nervously around)* Peanuts... A trail of peanuts... Leading in here.

**EDNA:** *(Puzzled)* That's strange.... Me too.

*(JACK has a delighted smile on his face.)*

**SARAH:** I'll phone the Police.

*(SARAH picks up the phone as the curtain falls.)*

## ACT III Scene 2

*(It is half an hour later. JACK and JILLY sit together on the settee. JACK has his arm round her. They look contented.)*

**JILLY:** Thank God that's all over.
**JACK:** If only I'd remembered before.
**JILLY:** If only I'd *known* before.
**JACK:** How could you have known?
**JILLY:** I don't mean about Walter. I mean about you.
**JACK:** *(Puzzled)* What about me?
**JILLY:** Walter said all you ever wanted was a nice quiet business...
**JACK:** Yes. So?
**JILLY:** ...and me. If only I'd known.
**JACK:** We made quite a mess of our marriage, didn't we?

*(JILLY nods with a long sigh.)*

**JILLY:** *(Sadly)* Too late now.
**JACK:** 'Fraid so.
**JILLY:** When d'you have to go back?
**JACK:** As soon as I found my killer, they said.
**JILLY:** I'll miss you, Jack.
**JACK:** I'll miss you too, Jilly.

*(They kiss.)*

**JILLY:** I nearly felt something then. *(A pause.)* How do you do it? Go back, that is.
**JACK:** I just concentrate hard and off I go.
**JILLY:** God, I'll miss you. Why couldn't you have been like this when you were alive?
**JACK:** One of life's great travesties, my love.
**JILLY:** Can I watch you go?
**JACK:** I suppose so. I don't know.
**JILLY:** Goodbye, my love.

*(They kiss again.)*

**JACK:** We'll meet again, Jilly... I know we will... One day.

*(They break apart. JILLY suppresses a tear as JACK closes his eyes and starts to concentrate. The lights start to dim slowly. When the lights are quite dim they suddenly snap back on. JACK's eyes snap open.)*

**JACK:** *(Decisive)* I'm not going!
**JILLY:** *(Taken aback)* What!? Can you do that?

## Wait Until The Ghost Is Clear

**JACK:** I've no idea! But if they want me, they'll have to come and get me. If *you* want me, that is.

**JILLY:** *(Excited)* Of course I do!

**JACK:** Won't people think you're mad talking to no-one?

**JILLY:** I don't care! For all I know I'm dreaming anyway, but if I am I want it to go on forever.

*(JILLY stands, goes to the phone and starts to dial.)*

**JACK:** Who are you calling?

**JILLY:** Sarah.

**JACK:** You can't tell her! You can't tell anyone. She was suspicious enough about the peanuts.

**JILLY:** *(Waiting for an answer)* I'm not going to tell her. I'm going to ask her where she buys her underwear. It's time you and I started living.

*(JACK rubs his hands lustily together as THE CURTAIN FALLS.)*

**The End**

### Wait Until The Ghost Is Clear
### Stage Set

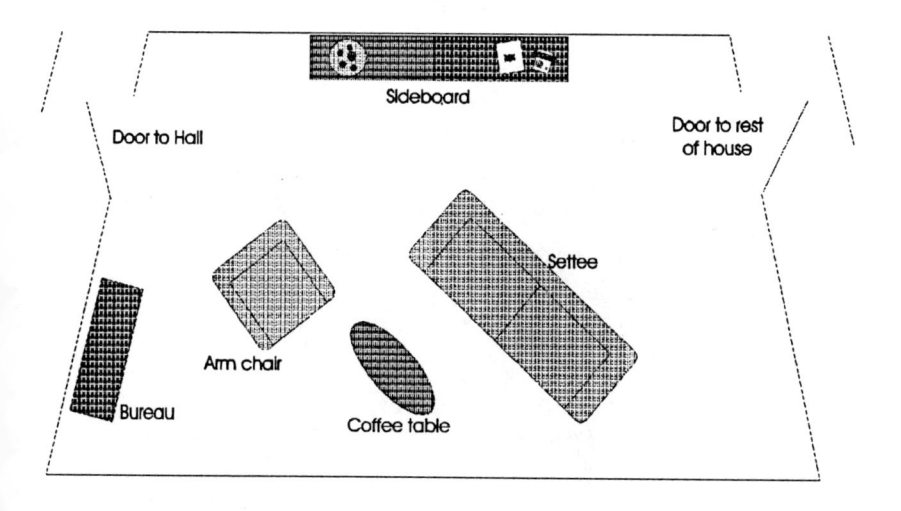

## Furniture & Properties

On Stage -
- Settee *(down L)*
- Armchair *(down R)*
- Coffee table *(down C)*
    - On it:-
        - Bowl of peanuts
- Sideboard *(up C)*
    - On it:-
        - Bottle of gin
        - Bottle of whisky
        - Bottle of tonic
        - Other bottles
        - Ornaments
        - Telephone
        - Pen
    - *In sideboard -*
        - Accounts books
- Wall mirror *(up L)*

### ACT I

- Newspaper
- Hair dryer *(SARAH, off R)*
- Handbag *(SARAH)*
- Wallet of photos *(SARAH, in her bag)*
- Hair dryer *(JILLY, off L)*
- Three TESCO carrier bags *(EDNA, off R)*
- Revolver *(JACK, off L)*
- Cleaning cloth *(JACK, off L)*
- Bunch of keys *(EDNA, in her pocket)*
- Five assorted suitcases *(JACK, off R)*
- Three carrier bags *(JACK, off R)*
- Wristwatch *(JACK)*

### ACT II

- Newspaper *(On the table)*
- Tray
    - On it:-
        - Teapot

Milk jug
Two cups and saucers
Note book and pen *(INSPECTOR JAMES, in her pocket)*
Cup *(SARAH, off L)*
Teapot *(SARAH, off L)*
Glass of water and two tablets *(SARAH, off L)*

## ACT III Scene 1

Towel *(SARAH)*
Spider *(JACK)*
Packet of stockings *(SARAH)*
Revolver *(WALTER, in his jacket)*
Frying pan *(EDNA, off L)*

## EFFECTS PLOT
## ACT I

**CUE 1: Doorbell rings** *(off R)*

    Cue:- after

**JACK:**      O.K! O.K! I promise!

**CUE 2: Doorbell rings** *(off R)*

    Cue:- after

**JACK:**      I'm going to the loo.

**CUE 3: Front door opens** *(off R)*

    Cue:- after JILLY exits R.

**CUE 4: Front door slams** *(off R)*

    Cue:- after SARAH and JILLY exit R.

**CUE 5: Doorbell rings** *(off R)*

    Cue:- after

**JACK:**      No, don't worry. I won't be pointing it at your mother.

**CUE 6: Front door opens** *(off R)*

    Cue:- after

**JACK:**      ...Devil!?

**CUE 7: Telephone rings**

    *Cue:- after*

**EDNA:**      Another *cowboy*! Playing with guns.

**CUE 8: Doorbell rings** *(off R)*
    Cue:- after

**JACK:**    It's well-made.

**CUE 9: Door opens and closes** *(off R)*
    Cue:- after JILLY exit R.

**CUE 10: Door opens and closes** *(off R)*
    Cue:- after WALTER exits following:-

**JILLY:**    'Bye, Walter. Close the door on your way out.

**CUE 11: Door opens and closes** *(off R)*
    Cue:- after EDNA exits following:-

**JACK:**    Take your time.

**CUE 12: Clattering noise** *(off R)*
    Cue:- after

**JACK:**    I have. I'll do it in a minute. I'm not exactly looking forward to it.

**CUE 13: Lights black out**
    *Cue:-* after JILLY reaches the door R.

**CUE 14: Single gunshot**
    *Cue:-* after

**JILLY:**    Mum...? Is that you?

## ACT II

**CUE 15: Doorbell rings** *(off R)*
    Cue:- after

**SARAH:**    I'm only going to the kitchen. I'll be back before you know it.

**CUE 16: Door opens and closes** *(off R)*
    Cue:- after SARAH exits following:-

**SARAH:**    You sit down. I'll go.

**CUE 17: Lights snap off**
    *Cue:-* as JILLY operates the switch following:-

**JILLY:**    I said "Mum...? Is that you?" and the lights went out, like this...

**CUE 18: Lights snap on**
    *Cue:-* as JILLY operates the switch following:-

**JILLY:** No. They just went off. Then there was the shot. I think I screamed. Then the lights came on again and...

**CUE 19: Lights snap off**

*Cue:-* as JILLY operates the switch following:-

**JILLY:** I don't believe this! I'm going mad.

**CUE 20: Lights snap on**

*Cue:-* as JILLY operates the switch following:-

**JACK:** Oi! Turn those lights on!

### ACT III Scene 1

**CUE 21: Telephone rings**

*Cue:-* after

**JILLY:** Sarah! No...!

**CUE 22: Doorbell rings** *(off R)*

Cue:- after

**JILLY:** Ohhh!

**CUE 23: Doorbell rings** *(off R)*

Cue:- after

**SARAH:** Mum's the word.

**CUE 24: Door opens and closes** *(off R)*

Cue:- after JILLY exits following:-

**JACK:** I promise. Now go and answer the door. I'd go myself, but whoever it is may not want to see me... Even if they could.

**CUE 25: Single gunshot**

*Cue:-* As SARAH knocks WALTER with the door L following:-

**WALTER:** I'm sorry, Jilly. You know too much.

**CUE 26: Lights gradually dim then suddenly snap back on**

*Cue:-* Some time after

**JACK:** We'll meet again, Jilly. I know we will. One day.

# New Playwrights' Network

This exciting project was launched in January 1972. Many of the major county and borough libraries accept quotas of new, full-length and one act stage plays which are included in their central collections for use by amateur dramatic societies for play reading purposes with a view to possible performances. Each play published has been approved by a distinguished panel of readers who have specialised knowledge of theatre requirements. Our aim is to publish high quality plays to enable NPN to compete successfully with products from the West End. NPN offers the best package deal ever made available to the talented playwright. Keep in touch with your local library!

Ask for **NPN** plays by name.

Contact us for details of our latest catalogues.

**New Playwrights' Network**

# WAIT UNTIL THE GHOST IS CLEAR
### a comedy by ian hornby

Jack's marriage to Jilly is not a happy one. His business is in trouble. Mother-in-law Edna is coming to stay. What else can go wrong?

Jack is cleaning his gun ready to go to the pistol club with his friend and partner Walter when suddenly the lights go out and there is a shot and a scream.

The police suspect Jilly of the murder. Things get worse when it is discovered someone had recently taken out a large life policy on Jack. In desperation Jilly's friend Sarah - who Jack used to find deperately attractive - suggests they try to recreate the crime. As the lights come back on, there is Jack as large as... *life*!????

Jack and Jilly do their best to discover the culprit - despite Jack being distracted by Sarah's presence - and eventually it is time he is laid to rest... except he doesn't want to go!

0863193323

ISBN N° 0 86319 332 3